REUTERS Global News Feed

ロイターニュースが伝える世界の今

Kobayashi Toshihiko　Bill Benfield

photographs by

ロイター

iStockphoto

DVD / Streaming Materials

Unit 1 : © ロイター

Unit 2 : © ロイター / Courtesy “GOMIHIROI SAMURAI”

Unit 3 ～ Unit 15 : © ロイター

StreamLine

Web 動画・音声ファイルのストリーミング再生について

CD マーク及び Web 動画マークがある箇所は、PC、スマートフォン、タブレット端末において、無料でストリーミング再生することができます。下記 URL よりご利用ください。再生手順や動作環境などは本書巻末の「Web 動画のご案内」をご覧ください。

https://st.seibido.co.jp

音声ファイルのダウンロードについて

CD マークがある箇所は、ダウンロードすることも可能です。下記 URL の書籍詳細ページにあるダウンロードアイコンをクリックしてください。

https://www.seibido.co.jp/ad716

Reuters Global News Feed

リンガポルタのご案内

リンガポルタ連動テキストをご購入の学生さんは、
「リンガポルタ」を無料でご利用いただけます！

本テキストで学習していただく内容に準拠した問題を、オンライン学習システム「リンガポルタ」で学習していただくことができます。PCだけでなく、スマートフォンやタブレットでも学習できます。単語や文法、リスニング力などをよりしっかり身に付けていただくため、ぜひ積極的に活用してください。

リンガポルタの利用にはアカウントとアクセスコードの登録が必要です。登録方法については下記ページにアクセスしてください。

https://www.seibido.co.jp/linguaporta/register.html

本テキスト「Reuters Global News Feed」のアクセスコードは下記です。

7311-2049-1231-0365-0003-0083-HG9E-Q4R5

・リンガポルタの学習機能（画像はサンプルです。また、すべてのテキストに以下の4つの機能が用意されているわけではありません）

●多肢選択

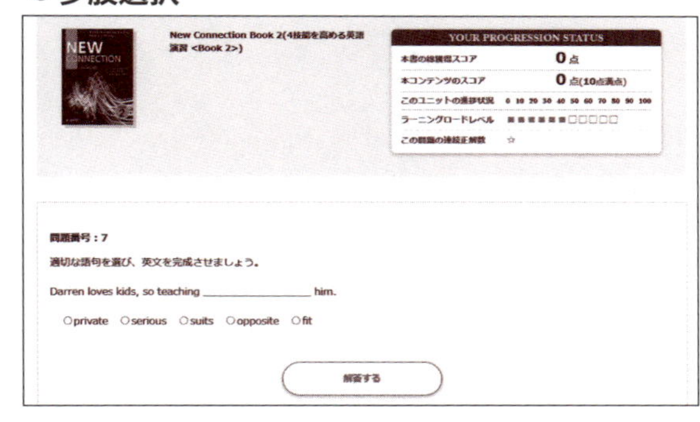

●空所補充（音声を使っての聞き取り問題も可能）

●単語並びかえ（マウスや手で単語を移動）

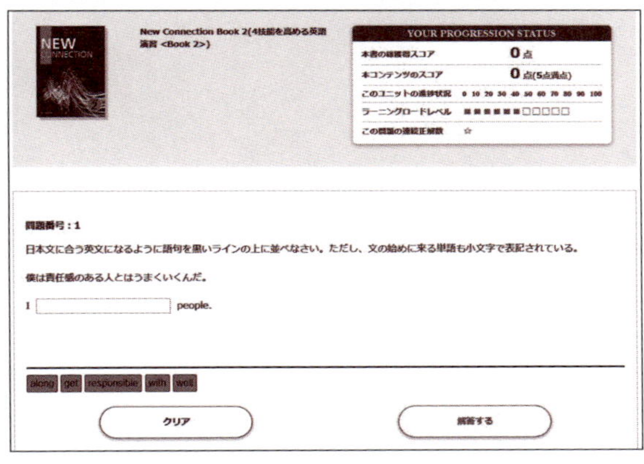

●マッチング（マウスや手で単語を移動）

Preface

最近、「ロイター通信によりますと」というフレーズを耳にしない日はないぐらい、ロイターのニュース配信が急速に拡大しています。主要な外国メディアであるテレビ、ラジオ、ネットニュース、英字新聞・雑誌などでも、ロイターから配信された（各報道機関に販売された）記事が多く見られます。そして、この歴史あるロイターのニュースレポートを大学の教材として活用できる時がついに来ました。本書は、ロイターの配信動画を題材にした教材であり、その機会をいただけたことを著者共々深く感謝するところです。

通信社 (news agency) とは、新聞などの媒体を持たず、取材したニュースリソースを新聞社や雑誌社、またはネット媒体に提供する企業です。ロイターは、欧州、アフリカ、ユーラシア、アジア、北米、中米、南米、オセアニアなど全世界に記者を配置し、日々映像、音声、記事を発信しています。本書では、世界中から集めた記事の中から大学生に興味深い内容と思われるものを教材として厳選し、15 章の構成で編成しています。

本書は、リスニング、スピーキング、リーディング、ライティングの4技能に加え、語彙力と文法力も向上させるために、さまざまなタスク（作業）が用意されています。授業ではニュースレポートの内容を理解し、コメントし、議論するだけでなく、学期中や授業終了後も、受講者それぞれが積極的に世界の出来事に関心を持ち、ネットニュースや英字新聞・雑誌、テレビ、ラジオなどのメディアから情報を収集しながら英語力を高め、さらにメディアリテラシーを高めていただければと存じます。

多くの大学生にとって、教室で英語を学ぶ機会は限られているため、その後は自分自身で英語学習を進めていかなければなりません。ネットが普及する前は、それは大変な苦労と費用と時間がかかることでしたが、現在の ICT の時代では非常に効率的に比較的短時間で語学を習得できる環境が整っています。本書を通じて、英語の情報にいつでもどこでもアクセスし、英語力を向上させ続ける自律的な英語学習者になっていただければ幸いです。

著者

ロイター本社

本書の目的と特長

本書は、検定教科書など語彙や構文が調整された教科書で英語を学んできた学習者が、初めてオーセンティックな（本物の、生の）英語レポートに接するための橋渡しを目指した4技能統合型の英語総合教材です。初めてオーセンティックな英語に触れる学習者がスムーズに慣れていけるように、ロイターが配信する原音だけでなく、従来のナレーターが朗読した音源も併用できるようにタスクを構成しています。

本書は以下の特長を有します。

1. オーセンティックな教材

現実の世界で、もっとも学習者が将来接すると考えられる英語ニュースに触れ、国際社会の今を見る、聞く、読む、書く、話すスキルをバランス良く上達できるようにしました。ロイターが24時間配信する、英語学習者用に調整されていないオーセンティックな英語音声に触れることで実用英語の運用能力の向上を目指します。ただし、検定教科書からオーセンティックなニュースリソースに触れる過渡期の学習者を対象とすることを念頭に、ロイターのビデオのそのままの音声を聞いて行うタスクに加え、従来にあるプロのナレーターの音源を使用したタスクやロイターからの配信動画に関連した英語母語話者が書き下ろした学習者用に調整された英文エッセイのリーディングを含めるなど、調整された教材から生の教材へのスムーズな移行ができるように工夫されています。

2. 4技能のバランスの取れたタスク構成

リスニング→リーディング→ライティング→スピーキングの順にタスクが構成されており、4技能のバランス良い学習が図れるように作られています。ロイターから配信された動画と選定された静止画を活用し、視聴、聴解、記述、会話という言語行動の流れを授業で実現できるように工夫されています。学習者はそれぞれのトピックに関する現実の世界のレポートにリスニングタスクを通じて触れ、さらに関連した書き下ろし英文を読んでその内容を深く洞察した上で、自分の意見を英文で書くタスクを行うことで、自分の考えを整理し、発信するための表現を学びます。また、それをインタビューや対話を通じて口頭で発信するスピーキング技能の向上も目指しています。ライティングは数分のスピーチ・プレゼンテーション用の原稿として、しっかりとした内容のメッセージを簡潔にまとめ上げ、最終ステップでそれを口頭発表用に推敲して教室で発表する流れになっています。

3. 世界の状況を理解し、人類の英知を学ぶ

将来の日本社会と世界の発展と幸福に貢献できる人材の養成を念頭に置き、学生の知的好奇心を刺激し、世界の諸問題についての意識を高めるために、「社会生活と文化」「ビジネスと消費生活」「健康と医学」「科学とテクノロジー」「野生動物と環境」の五大分野にそれぞれ3つのニュースレポートを当てはめ構成されています。本書で使用されている英語レポートをきっかけに、特定の分野への関心が喚起され、より詳細な情報を入手し知識を獲得することで、人類の英知に触れることが期待されています。それによって、より多くの関連した語彙学習の必要性を肌で感じ、授業で扱う語彙項目に加えて自律的な語彙習得も目指します。

本書の構成と使い方

PHASE 1 *WARM UP*

Photo Description

Look at the photo below and choose the sentence that best describes it.

写真描写

ビデオの中の1シーンの静止画を見て、その状況をもっとも正確に表す英文をひとつ選んでください。英文に不明語句が含まれている場合は辞書等で調べてから判断してください。

Vocabulary Preview

Choose the Japanese equivalent for each of the following English words or phrases.

語彙予習

ビデオの中で使用されている語句の中で比較的難易度の高い語句を 10 選んであります。それぞれ意味を表す和文のアルファベット（a ～ j）を空欄に書き入れてください。聞き取りのために紹介しているので、活用した、そのままの形で載せてあります。過去形の動詞を現在形にしたり、複数形の名詞を単数形に直してはいません。ただし、三単現の s が付いた形で聞こえる一般動詞や現在分詞は原形で載せています。

PHASE 2 *VIEWING & LISTENING*

Listening for Comprehension: Q&A

Watch the video and answer the following question.

質疑応答

ビデオの中で語られている内容について、比較的大まかな内容の設問が与えられています。ビデオを一度または数回見て設問の答えとなる部分に注意を傾けて聞き取って、英文で解答してください。また、このタスクの最中は STEP 5 にある英文スクリプトが目に入らないように注意してください。

Listening for Comprehension: Multiple Choice

Watch the video again and choose the best answer for each of the following questions.

多義選択

ビデオの中で語られている内容について、具体的な内容の聞き取りをする設問が与えられています。ビデオの音声を聞いて最適な選択肢を選んでください。同様に、このタスクの最中は STEP 5 にある英文スクリプトが目に入らないように注意してください。

Listening for Perception: Word Choice & Fill-in-the-Blanks

Listen to the following part and choose the words you hear or fill in the blanks.

空欄穴埋め

適切な間隔で語彙選択と空欄穴埋め（すべて 1 語）のスペースが設けられています。ビデオの音声を聞き取りやすくするためにアメリカ人の英語母語話者が朗読し直した音源を聞いて聞き取れた語句を選ぶか空欄に書き入れてください。音声を一度または数度、場合によっては特定の箇所を繰り返し何度も聞いてください。単語の選択は、三単現の s、名詞の単数・複数の s、15 と 50 などの聞き分けが微妙な語を中心に並べられています。冠詞の選択は、何も入らない場合 x を選んでください。また、STEP 2 で紹介された語句や数字を空欄にしてあります。知ったばかりの語句をすぐに音声で聞き取り着実に覚えることを狙っています。数字は、実生活の中で正確に聞き取らなければならない場面に遭遇することが考えられるので特に注意して聞き取るようにしてください。

Synchro-Reading

Listen to the recording and read the following passage silently to understand what is said.

シンクロ黙読

ビデオの内容に関連したイギリス人著者が書き下ろした270語前後の英文を、アメリカ人の英語母語話者による朗読を聞きながら黙読します。聞こえた位置に目線を合わせるように読み進めてください。途中で不明な語句があっても目線の移動を止めることなく先に進めてください。これは、英文を早く読み、多読をする学習習慣を形成するための準備となる訓練であり、内容の理解が主たる目的ではありません。一度聞きながら黙読した後に、今度は以下のタスクを行う際には与えられた時間内に自分のペースで精読してください。

Vocabulary View

Choose the definition or synonym for each of the following English words or phrases.

語彙復習

英文の中で使用されている語句の中で比較的難易度の高い語句を10選んであります。その意味を表す英文の定義または同義語のアルファベット（a ～ j）を空欄に書き入れてください。STEP 2ではビデオの音声の聞き取りを容易にするために、動詞の過去形や名詞の複数形などそのままの形で載せてあり、また和訳を選ぶようになっていますが、このステップでは、すでに読んでいる英文の中から選んだ語句であり、また定義文の形を統一するために、時制に関わらず、動詞は原形にしてあります。また、名詞も単複関わらず単数形で載せてあります。不明語句は英文を見て前後関係から意味を推測してください。わかりやすいものから選択して、辞書やスマホ等は使わないでください。

Reading Comprehension & Lexicogrammar: Word Choice

Choose (a)-(d) to complete each statement in a grammatically correct sentence so that it matches the content of the passage.

語彙選択

本文の内容に一致し、かつ語彙文法的にもっとも適切な語句を記号で選んでください。意味が近い選択肢が複数ありますが、その空欄の後にある単語の品詞や活用形から判断して文法的に不適切な選択肢は排除し、文法的知識を活かしてタスクを完成させてください。英文の内容の理解力、語彙力、文法力の3つが同時に求められるタスクです。

Best Summary

Choose the best summary.

要約文選択

本文の内容をもっともよく表した英文を5つの中から選んでください。正解以外の英文には本文の内容と異なる記述があったり、周辺的な情報しか含んでいないものがあります。このタスクは特定の長さの情報を読んで、要旨を他人に文面や口頭で端的に伝える訓練になります。

Step 10 Free Writing & Interviewing

Write your answer for each of the following questions and then ask each other each of the following questions below.

自由英作文&インタビュー

ビデオの内容 (A) および英文エッセイ (B) に関して自分自身の考えを表明するための英文の設問があります。まず、設問 (A) (B) についてよく考えながら簡潔に英文を書いてください。それから、(A) (B) のそれぞれにある3つの英文の質問をペアワークやグループワークで質問し合ってください。関連した質問なども加えてより自由な対話に発展させてください。これは口頭で行うものなので、書き取りなどを行わずに、しっかりと相手の目を見ながら対話するように努めてください。

Step 11 Template Essay Writing & Oral Presentation

Follow the template and write on the topic below and read it aloud in pairs or groups.

談話展開型小論文&プレゼンテーション

ビデオの内容や英文エッセイに関連した質問があります。既に用意されている英文の型に合わせて一定の長さの英語の長文を書いてください。STEP 10 のタスクで頭の中で整理された情報をしっかりとまとめた上で英文を書いてください。完成したらペアワークまたはグループワークで音読するか、できれば丸暗記して自分の意見を口頭で発表してください。

Step 12 Free Discussion

Listen to/read the model dialog and talk freely with your partner using the following question.

自由討論

ビデオの内容や英文エッセイに関連した質問があります。その質問を第一声にしてペアワーク、グループワーク、クラスワークで英語で討論してください。

Model Dialogs

対話例

参考の対話として、肯定的および否定的な対話の流れを想定したモデルダイアローグが提示されているので、朗読した音声を聞いて討論の流れを把握してください。ただし、このモデル対話はあくまでも参考程度にして、自分自身のオリジナルのメッセージを一定時間英語で発信してください。討論中に参考となる表現集を次にまとめてあるので討論の前や最中に参考にして使うようにしてください。

Useful Patterns for Writing & Speaking

ライティング&スピーキングに役立つ表現集

各ユニットのビデオスクリプト、エッセイ本文、タスクの選択肢等で使用されている英文の定型枠(パターン)の中からライティングとスピーキングに活用できるもの及び関連表現を10項目選んで掲載しています。適時参考にしてください。また、テキスト全体を通して、将来役立ちそうな表現を見つけたらマークしておき、自分自身の発信用のフレームワークとして構築してください。

CONTENTS

Female Rickshaw Pullers Wow Tourists in Japan

人力車の魅力 女性が引く人力車に外国人旅行者が大喜び

Have you ever ridden in a rickshaw? The video features a young female rickshaw puller popular among foreign tourists around the Kaminarimon area of Sensoji Temple in Tokyo. Observe her at work and discover the charm of rickshaws. The essay describes the history of rickshaws around the world and shows how they have developed or adjusted to modern life. Express your experiences with and/or opinions on this traditional yet new vehicle.

PHASE 1 *WARM UP*

Step 1 Photo Description

Look at the photo below and choose the sentence that best describes it.

1. One of the male rickshaw pullers in front is wearing a cap and a headband.
2. Some male rickshaw pullers are talking to some female ones.
3. All of the rickshaw pullers are looking ahead.
4. One of the rickshaw pullers is leaving the room.

Step 2 Vocabulary Preview

Choose the Japanese equivalent for each of the following English words or phrases.

1. rickshaw puller ______	a. 歓喜させる (=to impress someone very much)
2. wow ______	b. 極端に、非常に (=very; greatly; highly; terribly)
3. shine ______	c. 人力車の車夫
4. extremely ______	d. 輝く、活躍する (=to show great ability in an activity)
5. went through ______	e. 新入社員、新人 (=new employee)
6. quit ______	f. 案内する (=to show the way)
7. hang ______	g. 経験（体験）した (=experienced)
8. guide ______	h. 成功する (=to achieve the disired)
9. succeed ______	i. 辞める (=to stop working; to leave a company)
10. recruit ______	j. コツ (=knack)

PHASE 2 VIEWING & LISTENING

Step 3 Listening for Comprehension: Q&A

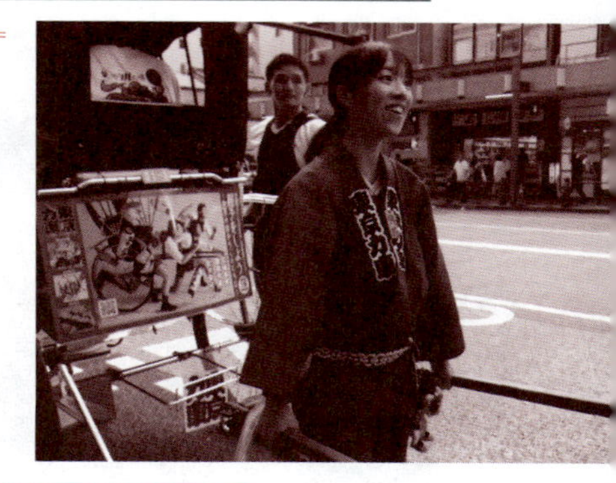

Watch the video and answer the following question. WEB動画 DVD (Time 01:51)

Q: How does the female rickshaw puller describe her job?

A: ....

....

Step 4 Listening for Comprehension: Multiple Choice

Watch the video again and choose the best answer for each of the following questions.

Q1: What trouble did the woman experience?

A. She damaged the rickshaw. **B.** She was unable to pull the rickshaw.
C. She dropped the rickshaw. **D.** Her rickshaw was stolen.

Q2: What is the approximate proportion of female pullers working for Tokyo Rickshaw?

A. 10% **B.** A quarter **C.** 30% **D.** A half

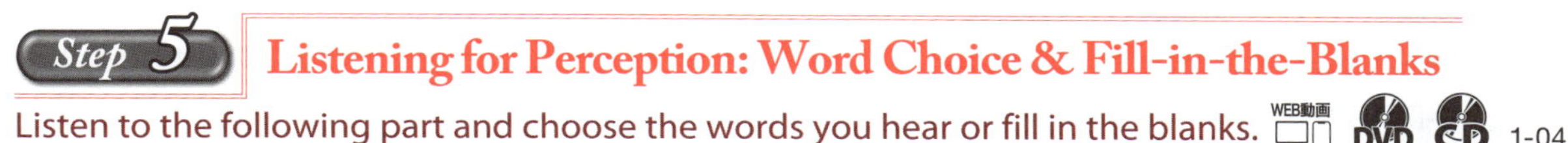

Step 5 Listening for Perception: Word Choice & Fill-in-the-Blanks

Listen to the following part and choose the words you hear or fill in the blanks. WEB動画 DVD CD 1-04

Narrator: Yuka Akimoto carries tourists on a black, two-wheeled cart to enjoy the [1](sites/sights) in the Asakusa district – one of Japan's most popular tourism spots.

Yuka Akimoto, Rickshaw puller: People usually think that [2](__________) rickshaws is a job for men, but I think it's a wonderful job that women can [3](__________) in as well. Every day I work like this with a smile. It's a [4](real/really) fun job. 5

Narrator: The cart can weigh up to [5](__________) pounds or about 250 kilograms and pullers walk or run an average of [6](__________) miles a day.

Yuka Akimoto, Rickshaw puller: I have zero [7](experience/experiences) with sports so pulling the rickshaw was extremely difficult for me. At first, I went through a lot of [8](trouble/troubles) such as dropping the rickshaw. There were many times when I 10 thought about [9](__________). But now I'm getting the [10](__________) of it, and I can pull the rickshaw. I really enjoy talking to our customers, taking photos for them, and [11](__________) them around. I want to keep working for as long as possible.

Narrator: The most popular drivers make over $[12](__________) a month.

Asli Turkseven, Tourist: In [the]* start I cannot believe she will carry us. But in the end, 15 I'm really happy to see the women [13](succeed/succeeding/succeeds) in this job. So I'm really happy.

Narrator: Akimoto's employer, Tokyo Rickshaw, hires [14](__________) pullers – about a third are women. They say they are actively seeking more female [15](recruit/recruits).

* [the] 文法的には定冠詞が必要だが、話者の音声を優先

PHASE 3 *LISTENING & READING*

Step 6 Synchro-Reading

1-05

Listen to the recording and read the following passage silently to understand what is said.

Rickshaws were once a common form of urban transportation in Asian cities. In the 19th century, Japan was the first country to put them into widespread use, and they became a common sight in the streets of major cities such as Tokyo (especially in Asakusa), Kyoto, and Otaru. They were so popular that other Asian countries soon 5 adopted them. However, as the 20th century progressed, the sight of poor drivers pulling well-off passengers through the streets came to be viewed as a symbol of poverty and exploitation, and the vehicles gradually disappeared. The last place where human-pulled rickshaws were in widespread use was the Indian city of Kolkata until city authorities banned them in 2006.

10 But far from dying out, rickshaws have made a comeback in a different form. Bicycle-style rickshaws can now be seen in cities all over the world, including several in the United States. Powered by bicycle pedals (sometimes assisted by a small motor) rather than by human muscle power alone, the modern-day version requires much less effort from the driver. In addition, rickshaws nowadays are also much safer and more 15 comfortable than the traditional ones. They are often equipped with features such as hydraulic brakes, good suspension, lighting, seat belts, and canopies to protect passengers from sunshine, wind, or rain.

Rickshaw companies are now trying to appeal primarily to tourists, who want a novel experience and the opportunity for some fun vacation photos. Nevertheless, many 20 local people are also coming to appreciate rickshaws because they are cheaper than taxis, can often avoid traffic jams, and are more environmentally friendly than cars or buses.

Step 7 Vocabulary View

1-06

Choose the definition or synonym for each of the following English words or phrases.

1. urban	______	a. little by little
2. sight	______	b. state of being poor
3. progress	______	c. covering, sunshade
4. well-off	______	d. chiefly; mainly; mostly
5. poverty	______	e. scene
6. exploitation	______	f. rich, wealthy
7. gradually	______	g. congestion
8. canopy	______	h. relating to cities
9. primarily	______	i. to move forward
10. jams	______	j. taking advantage of someone unfairly

Step 8 Reading Comprehension & Lexicogrammar: Word Choice

Choose (a)-(d) to complete each statement in a grammatically correct sentence so that it matches the content of the passage.

1. Japan was the first country where rickshaws went into ______ use.
   a. compulsory b. widespread c. temporary d. occasional

2. ______ the 20th century advanced, rickshaws became less and less popular.
   a. While b. During c. As d. Throughout

3. Some modern-day rickshaws have ______ canopies to shield passengers from the weather.
   a. protected b. protective c. protection d. protectable

4. Some local people are also starting to be attracted to rickshaws ______ tourists.
   a. as long as b. as far as c. as many as d. as well as

5. Modern-day rickshaws ______ traditional ones in the way they are powered.
   a. contrast to b. differ from c. compare with d. rank with

Step 9 Best Summary

Choose the best summary.

1. Rickshaws are replacing taxis and buses in many cities.
2. Rickshaws are popular again but only among tourists.
3. Modernized rickshaws are becoming popular in various cities.
4. Japan is mainly responsible for the renewed popularity of rickshaws.
5. Rickshaws are drawing more and more tourists to Japan.

PHASE 4 *WRITING & SPEAKING*

Step 10 Free Writing & Interviewing

Write your answer for each of the following questions and then ask each other each of the following questions below.

A. What do you think attracts foreign visitors to riding rickshaws?

....

....

....

1. Where in Japan would you like to be guided around in a rickshaw?
2. What kinds of foreign visitors do you think like to take a rickshaw ride?
3. How much do you think rickshaw pullers will charge you for a one-hour-ride?

B. What is the best way to get around when you go sightseeing?

....

....

....

1. Is it better to go sightseeing alone or as part of an organized group tour?
2. Is it important to have a local guide when you visit a famous tourist site?
3. Would you give a rickshaw driver a tip in addition to the normal fee?

Step 11 Template Essay Writing & Oral Presentation

Follow the template and write on the topic below and read it aloud in pairs or groups.

TOPIC: Should more cities in the world introduce rickshaws for tourists?

Introducing rickshaws would be good for some people because ....

....

....

....

However, other people might not be interested because ....

....

....

....

Personally, I feel that ....

....

....

....

Listen to/read the model dialog and talk freely with your partner using the following question.

QUESTION: Do you think a rickshaw business would be successful in your town?

Model Dialogs

Positive	Negative
A: Do you think a rickshaw business would be successful in your town? **B:** Definitely. **A:** Why do you think so? **B:** I see a lot of foreign tourists hanging around areas that have old buildings, but they have to walk such a long way. **A:** I see. Do you have any plans to start your own rickshaw business? **B:** Not sure, but I might start something to attract foreign tourists to my town.	**A:** Do you think a rickshaw business would be successful in your town? **B:** Definitely not. **A:** Why do you think so? **B:** There's no demand for the service. I've never seen any foreign visitors since I came to live in this town. **A:** Really? How about domestic tourists? **B:** No difference. Unfortunately, there are no tourist attractions at all. There aren't even many taxis available here.

Useful Patterns for Writing & Speaking from Unit 1

1	A came to be viewed as a symbol of B.	A は B の象徴として見られるようになりました。
2	What do you think attracts A to B?	A が B に魅了されるのはなぜだと思いますか。
3	What is the best way to ～ ?	～をするための最良（最善）の方法は何ですか。
4	Is it important to ～ ?	～をすることは大切なことですか。
5	Do you think ～ would be successful?	～は成功すると思いますか。
6	I see a lot of ～ .	～を多く見かけます。
7	Do you have any plans to ～ ?	～をする予定はありますか。
8	There is no demand for ～ .	～に対する需要がまったくありません。
9	Unfortunately, there are no ～ at all.	残念ながら～がまったくありません。
10	There aren't even many ～ available here.	ここでは～さえもあまり多くありません。

* [Useful Patterns for Writing & Speaking] の A と B は単数扱い

Tokyo's Trash-Picking Samurais Keep Streets Clean

1-10

街の美化 東京に侍姿のゴミ収集人現れる

What do you do when you see garbage on the road or see someone throw away garbage in public? How does this make you feel? In the video report, we look at a group of people in Japan who dress as samurai and pick up trash as a performance. Why do they do this? The essay introduces an app that may solve the problem of garbage on streets. Describe what you personally can do to solve this problem together with your experience of it.

PHASE 1 *WARM UP*

Photo Description

Look at the photo below and choose the sentence that best describes it.

1. The man is picking up trash from the ditch.
2. The man is carrying a basket on his back.
3. The man is sitting down on the sidewalk.
4. The man is leaning against the roadside fence.

Vocabulary Preview

1-11

Choose the Japanese equivalent for each of the following English words or phrases.

1. trash-picking ______
2. generation ______
3. prefecture ______
4. attention ______
5. aware ______
6. pick up ______
7. hardly ______
8. recognize ______
9. passerby ______
10. littering ______

a. 認識している (=conscious; informed)
b. 通行人 (=a person who passes by chance)
c. ほとんど〜しない (=scarcely)
d. 世代 (=age group)
e. 注意、注目、着目 (=notice; recognition)
f. ゴミ拾い
g. 〜を拾う (=take up; raise)
h. 判別できる (=to know what something is)
i. ポイ捨て
j. 都道府県

PHASE 2 *VIEWING & LISTENING*

Step 3 Listening for Comprehension: Q&A

Watch the video and answer the following question.

(Time 01:18)

Q: Why do they dress up as samurai to do trash-picking?

A: ....

....

Step 4 Listening for Comprehension: Multiple Choice

Watch the video again and choose the best answer for each of the following questions.

Q1: How many members of the man's company are working in the United States?

A. 0 **B.** 1 **C.** 2 **D.** 3

Q2: How often do they perform in samurai-style in Tokyo?

A. Every day **B.** Five times a week **C.** Once a week **D.** Every other week

Step 5 Listening for Perception: Word Choice & Fill-in-the-Blanks

Listen to the following part and choose the words you hear or fill in the blanks. WEB動画 DVD CD 1-12

Narrator: These trash-picking samurais are cleaning Tokyo's streets after Halloween. The volunteer group known as Gomihiroi Samurai was formed in [1](__________). It has since attracted a large [2](fan/fun) base, with nearly [3](__________) followers on TikTok.

Keisuke Naka: Right now we have three members in Tokyo, two in Los Angeles and also one member of [4](a/an/the/x) first generation in Hokkaido prefecture. Members in Tokyo dress up as samurai and perform trash-picking in [5](a/an/the/x) Japanese samurai style five times [6](a/an/the/x) week.

Narrator: Occasions such as Halloween leave a lot of trash as street drinking is common in bustling areas and tourist spots.

Keisuke Naka: If we can [7](__________) attention on the street, people who have no interest in the trash problem will become [8](__________) of it. There are many other volunteer groups [9](pick/picked/picking) up trash, but they are hardly recognized by passerby*.

Junya Kakihara: Normally I don't [10](__________), but after seeing what they did, I started paying attention to the [11](__________) issue and I would stop people from [12](__________) when they are about to do so.

* **[passerby]** 文法的には **passersby** が正しいが、話者の音声を優先

Step 6 Synchro-Reading

1-13

Listen to the recording and read the following passage silently to understand what is said.

During the 2022 Soccer World Cup in Qatar, TV viewers around the world saw something that astonished them. Just after the final whistle blew at the match between Japan and Costa Rica, Japanese fans began to meticulously pick up trash inside the stadium. This is not just something that Japanese people do in front of an international audience. Also, back home in Japan, it is expected that people will pick up their trash and take it home with them from public spaces like beaches or parks. This may explain the lack of public trash receptacles in Japan, something that foreign visitors find puzzling.

Despite the worthy efforts of Japanese citizens, the problem of trash disposal remains a huge problem all over the world. In spite of making huge efforts to recycle and dispose of waste, authorities are often unable to deal with the enormous volume of trash produced every day. As a result, much of this waste ends up being dumped illegally in city streets, fields, forests, rivers, and oceans, creating health hazards and destroying animal habitats.

For a long time, people concerned about the problem were at a loss as to how to deal with it. Now, technology is providing a possible solution. TrashOut is an environmental project that aims to map illegal dumping sites around the world and help citizens recycle more. If people come across an illegal trash dump, they can use the TrashOut mobile app to take a picture of it and report its location to environmental organizations or local authorities. With this information, city authorities or volunteers can organize a cleanup operation. The TrashOut app even enables the finders of the dump site to organize a cleanup event themselves.

Step 7 Vocabulary View

1-14

Choose the definition or synonym for each of the following English words or phrases.

1. astonish	______	a.	against the law
2. meticulously	______	b.	very hard or impossible to understand
3. receptacle	______	c.	natural home for an animal or plant
4. puzzling	______	d.	very big
5. enormous	______	e.	to dispose of something carelessly
6. dump	______	f.	with great care
7. hazard	______	g.	surprise greatly
8. habitat	______	h.	to find by chance
9. illegal	______	i.	container
10. come across	______	j.	danger

Step 8 Reading Comprehension & Lexicogrammar: Word Choice

Choose (a)-(d) to complete each statement in a grammatically correct sentence so that it matches the content of the passage.

1. International TV viewers were very surprised ________ Japanese fans picking up trash inside the stadium.
   a. to see b. saw c. seen d. to be seen

2. ________ authorities make huge efforts to clean up waste, the situation remains serious.
   a. Even b. Despite c. Even though d. However

3. When people come ________ an illegal trash dump, TrashOut enables them to photograph it.
   a. around b. across c. over d. through

4. ________ a result, a lot of illegal trash dumping takes place.
   a. For b. As c. By d. With

5. In Japan, people are ________ to take their trash home with them.
   a. strictly warned b. legally required
   c. sometimes requested d. usually expected

Step 9 Best Summary

Choose the best summary.

1. Japan is a world leader in environmental cleanup activities.
2. Illegal trash dumping is a problem we will never solve.
3. More and more people are joining environmental organizations.
4. Local authorities are using more environmentally friendly technology.
5. There is an app that makes it easier to locate and clean up trash.

Step 10 Free Writing & Interviewing

Write your answer for each of the following questions and then ask each other each of the following questions below.

A. What is the best solution for reducing garbage?

....

....

....

1. Are you interested in the issue of trash?
2. Do you pick up trash on the street when you see it?
3. When you see someone drop trash on the street, how do you feel?

B. Would you be likely to install the TrashOut app on your phone?

....

....

....

1. Would you ever volunteer to join an environmental cleanup effort?
2. Have you ever seen trash dumped in a beautiful spot?
3. Who is responsible for cleaning up trash – individuals, companies, or the government?

Step 11 Template Essay Writing & Oral Presentation

Follow the template and write on the topic below and read it aloud in pairs or groups.

TOPIC: What can individual people do to keep the environment clean?

One thing individual people can do to keep the environment clean is to ....

....

....

....

Not only that, but they can also ....

....

....

....

In conclusion, I think people should ....

....

....

....

Step 12 Free Discussion

1-15 ～ 17

Listen to/read the model dialog and talk freely with your partner using the following question.

QUESTION: Do you pick up trash when you see it lying on the ground?

Model Dialogs

Positive	Negative
A: Do you pick up trash when you see it lying on the ground? **B:** Not really. **A:** What do you mean? **B:** If it's something valuable, I may pick it up and take it home. **A:** Have you ever taken something home? **B:** Yes, I picked up a 500-yen coin yesterday, and I bought some soda with it.	**A:** Do you pick up trash when you see it lying on the ground? **B:** No way! It's dirty. It's not hygienic. **A:** How can you tell? **B:** I can't tell if it's safe or not. So I just won't touch anything that has been left on the ground. **A:** Okay, that makes sense.

Useful Patterns for Writing & Speaking from Unit 2

1	Despite the worthy efforts of A, the problem of B remains a huge problem all over the world.	A の価値ある努力にも関わらず、B は世界中でいまだに大問題です。
2	～ is a problem we will never solve.	～は今後も解決できない問題です。
3	There is an app that makes it easier to ～ .	～をするのをもっと容易にするアプリがあります。
4	What is the best solution for ～ ?	～の最良（最善）の解決策は何ですか。
5	Are you interested in the issue of ～ ?	～の問題に興味がありますか。
6	When you see someone ～ , how do you feel?	～をする人を見かけたらどう感じますか。
7	Would you be likely to ～ ?	～をしてみようとは思いませんか。
8	Would you ever volunteer to ～ ?	自ら進んで～をしてみようとは思いませんか。
9	Who is responsible for A, B or C?	A に対する責任があるのは B ですか、C ですか。
10	Do you A when you B?	B をする時は A をしますか。

Japan Says "Overtourism" Is Spoiling Mt. Fuji

1-18

オーバーツーリズム 観光客が殺到、富士山が過密状態に

Do you have problems with an excessive influx of visitors into your town? The video shows how Mt. Fuji, the world famous peak and symbol of Japan, has been flooded with overseas tourists, causing serious problems, including environmental ones. The essay focuses on the city of Venice in northeastern Italy, which has been struggling with extreme overtourism. Some solutions have been proposed and put into practice. How would you solve this problem if it should happen in your community or if it has already happened?

PHASE 1 *WARM UP*

Photo Description

Look at the photo below and choose the sentence that best describes it.

1. No one is wearing outdoor clothing in spite of the heavy rain.
2. Some climbers are holding ski poles while walking.
3. Everyone is empty-handed but carrying something on their back.
4. All are walking together, wearing light clothes.

Vocabulary Preview

1-19

Choose the Japanese equivalent for each of the following English words or phrases.

1. bins ______	a. 負荷、負担、圧迫 (=great or excessive demands)
2. iconic ______	b. 汚れた (=dirty; unclean)
3. symmetrical ______	c. ゴミ (=rubbish; waste)
4. strains ______	d. 有料道路
5. straddle ______	e. (土地を) またぐ
6. rife ______	f. いっぱいの (=widespread)
7. soiled ______	g. (左右) 対称の
8. litter ______	h. 名高い、象徴的な (=acting as a symbol)
9. toll road ______	i. ゴミ入れ (=dustbins イギリス英語/trash cans アメリカ英語)
10. drastic ______	j. 思い切った (=radical)

PHASE 2 *VIEWING & LISTENING*

Step 3 Listening for Comprehension: Q&A

Watch the video and answer the following question.

(Time 01:38)

Q: What are the problems being reported at Mt. Fuji?

A: ……………………………………………………………………………

……………………………………………………………………………

Step 4 Listening for Comprehension: Multiple Choice

Watch the video again and choose the best answer for each of the following questions.

Q1: According to the video, when was Mt. Fuji designated as a World Heritage site?

A. 5 years ago **B.** 7 years ago **C.** 10 years ago **D.** 12 years ago

Q2: What is the solution suggested for overtourism at Mt. Fuji?

A. Railway **B.** Entry fees **C.** I.D. check **D.** Body check

Step 5 Listening for Perception: Word Choice & Fill-in-the-Blanks

Listen to the following part and choose the words you hear or fill in the blanks.

1-20

Narrator: Long lines, overflowing [1](__________) and broken toilets...scenes you might expect at a [2](**county/country**) fair but maybe not Mt. Fuji, the iconic Japanese mountain, a sacred source of pride in the country for its [3](__________) form. However, a recent surge in inbound tourists after Japan reopened its borders has led to extreme levels of pollution and other [4](__________) on the country's tallest peak, authorities say. Here's Masatake Izumi, an official from Yamanashi, one of two prefectures that Fuji [5](__________).

Izumi: Many people are visiting Mt. Fuji and we appreciate that. But that is also leading to overtourism, with garbage and problems with the toilets [6](**resulted/resulting**) from the large number of people. We are now in a critical situation.

Narrator: Mt. Fuji was listed as [7](**a/an/the/x**) UNESCO World Heritage site a decade ago, which only boosted its popularity. Though that distinction came with conditions that Japan [8](**reduce/reduces/reduced**) overcrowding and environmental harm from visitors, overcrowding has only grown worse. The largest base station on the mountain saw four million visitors this summer, a [9](**15/50**)% jump from 2013. Social media has been rife with posts about [10](__________) bathrooms and mounds of litter on the hiking [11](**pass/paths**). Authorities say they are considering drastic measures to reduce the volume.

Izumi: [12](**A/An/The/x**) biggest cause of overtourism on Mt. Fuji is that the 5th station up the mountain can be easily reached by car. That means we need to control [13](**that/the**) access. However, since the Fuji Subaru Line toll road is also a prefectural road in Yamanashi, it [14](**will/would**) be difficult to regulate it. So we want to make a drastic change to replace the road with [15](**a/an/the/x**) mountain railway.

PHASE 3 *LISTENING & READING*

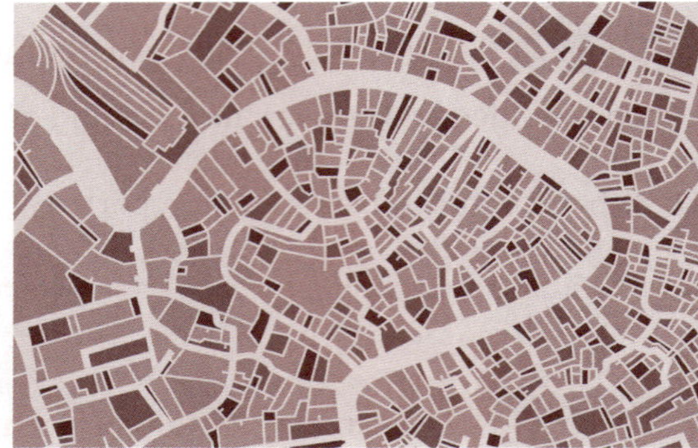

Synchro-Reading

1-21

Listen to the recording and read the following passage silently to understand what is said.

With its unique system of canals, mysterious narrow streets, and Renaissance buildings, Venice has always been a magnet for tourists. But the fragile city is now struggling to deal with the huge number of visitors that flock there every year. The numbers are quite hard to believe. Venice has about 55,000 permanent residents, yet it attracts 20 million visitors a year, or around 120,000 people per day.

One of the main causes of overtourism in Venice and other iconic cities is the rise in recent years of so-called low-cost carriers. The popularity of these budget airlines, which offer cheap flights to popular destinations, has led to a huge surge in tourist numbers.

Coastal cities such as Venice, Barcelona, and Amsterdam, however, face a further problem: regular visits from enormous cruise ships that can dock close to the city center. The large number of tourists who arrive in the city in this way contribute to the many problems caused by overtourism, including overcrowded historic sites, excessive trash on the streets, and strain on the local infrastructure. Because these tourists often sleep and take their meals on their cruise ship, they are essentially day trippers. Compared to visitors who actually stay in the city, they do not spend much money there and so bring minimal benefit to the local economy.

Recently, city authorities in Venice have tried to respond to the problem of overtourism. Measures include imposing an entry fee of 5 euro a day on tourists entering the city and restricting the places where the largest of the cruise ships can dock. Let us hope that this unique city can find a way to survive while allowing visitors to experience its charms and mystery.

Step 7 Vocabulary View

1-22

Choose the definition or synonym for each of the following English words or phrases.

1. fragile	______	a. to be partly responsible for
2. flock	______	b. to move or come together in large numbers
3. permanent	______	c. the goal of a journey
4. iconic	______	d. something that causes stress or difficulty
5. destination	______	e. sudden increase
6. surge	______	f. famous, recognized for being excellent
7. dock	______	g. (for a ship) to come alongside the shore
8. contribute to	______	h. lasting for a long time or for ever
9. strain	______	i. very small or slight
10. minimal	______	j. weak, easy to break

Step 8 Reading Comprehension & Lexicogrammar: Word Choice

Choose (a)-(d) to complete each statement in a grammatically correct sentence so that it matches the content of the passage.

1. Every year, millions of tourists are ______ to Venice.
   a. interested b. drawn c. visiting d. attracting

2. The number of tourists that visit Venice every year seems quite ______ .
   a. unthinkable b. unusual c. uncommon d. unbelievable

3. In some cities, overtourism ______ a combination of cheap airline tickets and gigantic cruise ships.
   a. is responsible for b. takes into account c. is the result of d. will cause

4. Cruise ship passengers do not contribute ______ to Venice's economy as conventional tourists.
   a. as much b. so many c. too few d. as little

5. Venice's authorities have taken various measures to ______ the problem of too many tourists.
   a. come up with b. dispose of c. deal with d. keep up with

Step 9 Best Summary

Choose the best summary.

1. Venice is trying to attract more cruise ship passengers to visit the city.
2. Overtourism causes several problems in Venice, which is trying its best to solve them.
3. As a way to solve problems of overtourism, Venice is thinking of banning cruise ships.
4. Venice's problems with overtourism are serious and are not found in other cities.
5. Venice has had problems with overtourism but will solve them soon.

Step 10 Free Writing & Interviewing

Write your answer for each of the following questions and then ask each other each of the following questions below.

A. What do you think attracts foreign visitors to Mt. Fuji?

....

....

....

1. Would you like to climb Mt. Fuji? Why or why not?
2. What other measures do you think should be taken to solve the problems at Mt. Fuji?
3. Do you think Mt. Fuji's popularity among inbound travelers will continue?

B. Do you think Venice is likely to solve the problems of overtourism in the near future? Why or why not?

....

....

....

1. Would you like to visit Venice? Why or why not?
2. Which do you like better, busy destinations with many tourists or quiet ones? Why?
3. Have you ever been bothered by huge numbers of tourists at public places such as railway or bus stations or seen them display bad manners?

Step 11 Template Essay Writing & Oral Presentation

Follow the template and write on the topic below and read it aloud in pairs or groups.

TOPIC: What are the positive or negative effects of large-scale tourism?

On the positive side, ...

....

....

....

On the negative side, however, ...

....

....

....

In sum, ...

....

....

....

Step 12 Free Discussion

CD 1-23 ～ 25

Listen to/read the model dialog and talk freely with your partner using the following question.

QUESTION: What do you think should be done to solve problems caused by overtourism?

Model Dialogs

Positive	Negative
A: What do you think should be done to solve problems caused by overtourism? **B:** We need to take some drastic measures. **A:** Such as? **B:** Impose a new high-rate tourist tax on visitors. **A:** Only for inbound tourists? **B:** No, for both domestic and international tourists. I believe this measure will work to discourage tourists from visiting overcrowded cities or sites. But it should exclude those visiting for business purposes.	**A:** What do you think should be done to solve problems caused by overtourism? **B:** I don’t think we need to take any action. **A:** What?! You really think so? **B:** Yes. I think people should be free to go wherever they like without any restrictions. **A:** But local residents are often complaining that overtourism is making daily life difficult for them. **B:** But it helps the local economy, doesn’t it? I’m sure they’ll get used to it eventually.

Useful Patterns for Writing & Speaking from Unit 3

1	What are the problems currently being reported at [in] ～ ?	～でいま報じられている問題は何ですか。
2	A has led to extreme levels of B.	A が B のレベルを極端に上げてしまったのです。
3	We want to make a drastic change to replace A with B.	A を B に変える思い切った改革をしたいのです。
4	One of the main causes of A is the rise in recent years of B.	A の主たる原因は近年 B が増えたからです。
5	Measures include ～ .	対策には～が含まれています。
6	What other measures do you think should be done to solve ～ ?	～の解決法は他に何があると思いますか。
7	Which do you like better, A or B?	A と B のどちらのほうが好きですか。
8	Have you ever been bothered by ～ ?	～に困ったことがありますか。
9	What do you think should be done to solve problems caused by ～ ?	～が原因で起きる問題をどう解決すべきであると思いますか。
10	I think people should be free to ～ wherever they like without any restrictions.	人には制限なくどこでも～をする自由があるべきであると思います。

China Issues Rules to Curb Gaming Spend

ビデオゲーム規制 | 中国でビデオゲームが規制される

Are you addicted to playing video games or do you know anyone who is? Online video games are very popular among young people everywhere, especially in China, where e-sports competitions are frequently held. The video reports on the Chinese government's regulations on game-play time and other practices. The essay focuses on a WHO report on gaming disorder. Talk about your own experience with video games and ideas on this issue.

PHASE 1 *WARM UP*

Photo Description

Look at the photo below and choose the sentence that best describes it.

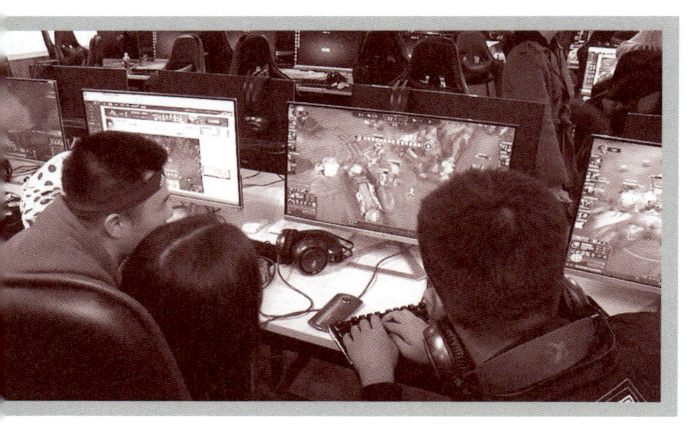

1. There are three young people playing a game remotely.
2. One of the people is operating a regular keyboard.
3. All three people are wearing headsets that cover their ears.
4. The man on the left is instructing the man on the right what to do.

Vocabulary Preview

Choose the Japanese equivalent for each of the following English words or phrases.

1. curb ______
2. regulators ______
3. rewards ______
4. consecutively ______
5. spook ______
6. deal a blow ______
7. cite ______
8. addiction ______
9. shrank ______
10. crackdown ______

a. 引用する (=to quote)
b. 中毒 (=dependency; dependence)
c. 弾圧、取り締まり (=clampdown)
d. 縮小した (=decreased)
e. 怖がらせる、ビビらせる (=to frighten)
f. 制限する、規制する (=to control or limit)
g. 規制当局
h. 痛手となる (=to give damage)
i. (ゲームの) リワード、報酬
j. 連続して (=in a row)

PHASE 2 VIEWING & LISTENING

Listening for Comprehension: Q&A

Watch the video and answer the following question. WEB動画 DVD (Time 01:11)

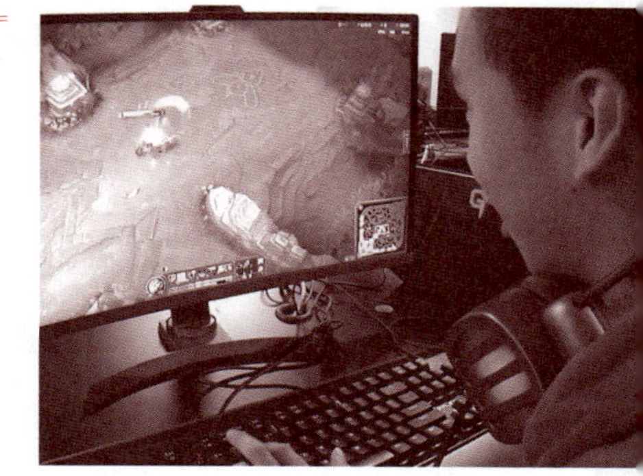

Q: What are the new rules?

A: ....

....

Step 4 Listening for Comprehension: Multiple Choice

WEB動画 DVD

Watch the video again and choose the best answer for each of the following questions.

Q1: Which company's shares fell more sharply, Tencent or NetEase?

A. Tencent B. NetEase C. No difference D. Not mentioned

Q2: What concerns are behind Beijing's tough line on video games?

A. National security B. Economy C. Health D. Not mentioned

Listening for Perception: Word Choice & Fill-in-the-Blanks

Listen to the following part and choose the words you hear or fill in the blanks. WEB動画 DVD CD 1-28

Narrator: China has made [1](strict/stricter) new rules for its multi-billion dollar gaming industry. Regulators want to [2](__________) spending and rewards that encourage video games. Online games will now effectively have spending [3](limit/limits) and face bans from giving [4](__________) to players if they log in every day. [5](__________) also can't be given to anyone who spends on [6](a/an/the/x) game for the first time, or if they spend several times on the game consecutively. The decision [7](__________) investors, and dealt a blow to the world's biggest games market, which returned to [8](grow/growth) this year. Shares in gaming giant Tencent were down as much as [9](16/60)% Friday, while its closest rival NetEase was down by a quarter. Beijing has taken a [10](tough/tougher) line on video games over the years. It set strict playtime limits for players younger than [11](__________) two years ago. It also suspended the approval of new video games for about eight months, [12](cited/citing) gaming addiction concerns. Last year was China's gaming industry's most difficult year on record, as total revenue [13](__________) for the first time. The crackdown formally ended in 2022 as [14](a/an/the/x) new game approvals resumed.

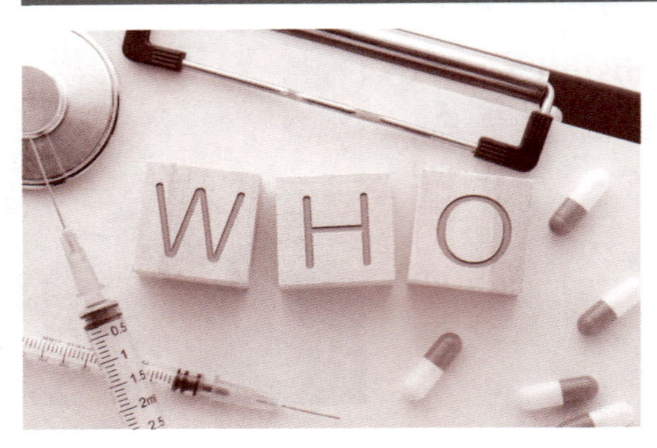

Synchro-Reading

1-29

Listen to the recording and read the following passage silently to understand what is said.

The World Health Organization (WHO) has a document called the International Classification of Diseases, which is a list of names, symptoms, and types of diseases. In 2018 it added a new disease to the list: gaming disorder, or an addiction to video games, which it classified as a mental disorder. According to the definition, people can be considered as having a gaming addiction if they are unable to control how much time they spend on gaming or if they prioritize gaming over regular daily activities such as studying, eating, or sleeping.

People can become addicted to gaming from a combination of reasons. On a psychological level, people can use games as a means of escapism, preferring to immerse themselves in the world of games rather than face the stresses and challenges of daily life. On a biological level, the mechanism of rewards built into games, such as rising through levels or earning points, can trigger the release of a chemical in the brain called dopamine, which creates feelings of pleasure. On a social level, players can often feel peer pressure from their friends in the gaming community to spend more time gaming.

Japan's Health, Labor and Welfare Ministry is concerned about the number of young people becoming addicted to gaming. It fears that it could lead many of them to become shut-ins, leading unproductive lives. There is an additional concern that excessive gaming can prevent young people from building strong interpersonal relationships and developing good work and study habits that will be important later in life. The problem is especially serious because Japan lacks trained therapists to counsel the increasing number of young people who find themselves in this position.

Step 7 Vocabulary View

1-30

Choose the definition or synonym for each of the following English words or phrases.

1. symptom	______	a.	to consider as most important
2. disorder	______	b.	a detailed explanation of what a word means
3. definition	______	c.	someone who never leaves their room
4. prioritize	______	d.	sign of an illness
5. combination	______	e.	a person of equal status
6. immerse	______	f.	two or more things together
7. trigger	______	g.	too much
8. peer	______	h.	to completely surround
9. shut-in	______	i.	to make something begin
10. excessive	______	j.	abnormal physical or mental condition

Step 8 Reading Comprehension & Lexicogrammar: Word Choice

Choose (a)-(d) to complete each statement in a grammatically correct sentence so that it matches the content of the passage.

1. In 2018, gaming disorder was added to the International Classification of Diseases, ______ is a WHO document.
   a. that　b. where　c. which　d. who

2. There is a combination of reasons why people become ______ to gaming.
   a. addict　b. addictive　c. addict　d. addicted

3. Pressure from friends, known as ______ pressure, can make people play games more intensely.
   a. peer　b. pair　c. pear　d. pier

4. Playing games too much can affect young people, preventing them ______ normally.
   a. to develop　b. from developing　c. in development　d. developed

5. Japan lacks trained therapists to ______ young people with gaming disorder.
   a. cancel　b. council　c. counsel　d. console

Step 9 Best Summary

Choose the best summary.

1. Japan and WHO are discussing the best way to prevent gaming addition.
2. It is difficult to identify the reasons why young people become addicted to gaming.
3. Gaming addiction is a serious problem and Japan's government is concerned about it.
4. Gaming addiction in Japan has led to an increase in the number of therapists.
5. If gaming addiction grows, WHO will likely recognize it as a disorder.

PHASE 4 *WRITING & SPEAKING*

Step 10 Free Writing & Interviewing

Write your answer for each of the following questions and then ask each other each of the following questions below.

A. What do you think about China's policy on gaming?

1. Do you think Japan should be as tough on gaming as China?
2. What do you think about the merits and demerits of Beijing's policy?
3. Do you think China will make tougher decisions on gaming in the future?

B. What do you think about gaming addiction?

1. How often do you play online video games? What are some of your favorite games?
2. Do you know anyone who seems to be addicted to gaming? How can you tell?
3. How do you think gaming addiction can be avoided or cured?

Step 11 Template Essay Writing & Oral Presentation

Follow the template and write on the topic below and read it aloud in pairs or groups.

TOPIC: What do you think the Japanese government should do about gaming?

In the first place, I think the Japanese government should ....

As an additional measure, I would suggest that ....

If the Japanese government did these two things, I believe that ....

Free Discussion

1-31 ～ 33

Listen to/read the model dialog and talk freely with your partner using the following question.

QUESTION: Do you think gaming should be limited?

Model Dialogs

Positive	Negative
A: Do you think gaming should be limited? **B:** Absolutely. **A:** Why do you think so? **B:** I'm really concerned about gaming addiction. I guess it seriously affects game players' health, especially their eyes and nervous systems. It could even affect their personality growth or development. **A:** So, you think our government should take a tough policy on gaming just like Beijing? **B:** Absolutely. We need it immediately.	**A:** Do you think gaming should be limited? **B:** Absolutely not. People should be free to do anything they like as long as they are responsible for their own health. **A:** But, do you think kids can control themselves? Don't you think parents should watch them closely and take care of their health? **B:** Well, that's none of the parents' concerns. Children have freedom. **A:** That's an interesting idea.

Useful Patterns for Writing & Speaking from Unit 4

1	It is difficult to identify the reasons why ～ .	～である理由を特定するには困難です。
2	A has led to an increase in the number of B.	A が原因で B の数が増えました。
3	What do you think about the merits and demerits of ～ policy?	～の方針のメリットとデメリットは何ですか。
4	Do you think A will make tougher decisions on B?	A は B に関してより厳しい決定を行うと思いますか。
5	Do you know anyone who seems to be addicted to ～ ?	～中毒と思われる人は誰か知っていますか。
6	How do you think ～ can be avoided?	～はどうすれば防げると思いますか。
7	Do you think ～ should be limited?	～は制限されるべきであると思いますか。
8	I'm really concerned about ～ .	～について非常に懸念しています。
9	People should be free to do anything they like as long as they are responsible for their own ～ .	自分自身の～に対して責任を持つ限り、人は好きなことは何でもして良いと思います。
10	Don't you think A should B?	A は B をするべきであると思いませんか。

McDonald's Gets a Taste for China Growth

 1-34

企業の海外進出 マクドナルドが中国で新店舗を増やす

Do you like fast food? While many foreign companies are withdrawing from the Chinese market, McDonald's, a major US fast food chain, is increasing the number of its stores there. Why is this? The essay depicts the management and history of the popular coffee chain Starbucks in Japan. For discussion and writing, describe your own experience with these chains and your concern about the possible effect of fast food on your health.

PHASE 1 *WARM UP*

Photo Description

Look at the photo below and choose the sentence that best describes it.

1. The McDonald's sign is attached to the top of a pagoda.
2. The McDonald's sign has three Chinese characters on it.
3. There are some birds on the top of the left pagoda.
4. A Chinese flag can be seen flying behind the McDonald's sign.

Vocabulary Preview

 1-35

Choose the Japanese equivalent for each of the following English words or phrases.

1. get a taste for ______
2. strike a deal to ______
3. ramp up one's stakes in ______
4. buy out ______
5. multinational corporations ______
6. pull back investments ______
7. geopolitical ______
8. capture higher demand ______
9. financial terms ______
10. value ______

a. 地政学的な
b. 多国籍企業
c. 評価額を付ける
d. より高い需要を獲得する
e. ～における出資比率を引き上げる
f. （契約上の）金銭的条件
g. （株式などを）買い上げる、買い取る
h. ～の味をしめる
i. ～する取引（契約） を行う
j. 投資を撤回する

PHASE 2 *VIEWING & LISTENING*

Step 3 Listening for Comprehension: Q&A

Watch the video and answer the following question.  (Time 01:07)

Q: Why is McDonald's expanding its business in China?

A: ....

....

Step 4 Listening for Comprehension: Multiple Choice 

Watch the video again and choose the best answer for each of the following questions.

Q1: How does McDonald's CEO describe the Chinese market in relation to his company?

A. its fast-growing market **B.** its fast-grown market
C. its fastest-growing market **D.** its fastest-grown market

Q2: Which country is McDonald's second largest market?

A. The United States **B.** China **C.** Japan **D.** Not mentioned

Step 5 Listening for Perception: Word Choice & Fill-in-the-Blanks

Listen to the following part and choose the words you hear or fill in the blanks. WEB動画 DVD CD 1-36

Narrator: McDonald's has got [1](a/an/the/x) taste for growth in China. The U.S. fast food giant says it has struck a deal to [2](__________) (__________) its stake in its Chinese business to [3](__________)%. The deal sees McDonald's buy out a [4](__________)% stake held by Carlyle investment group. The move is in sharp contrast to other multinational corporations. Many have pulled back [5](investment/investments) in China or even left the market altogether due to geopolitical and economic [6](worry/worries). But McDonald's chief executive Chris Kempczinski said Monday that he believed there was [7](no/not) better time to capture [8](high/higher) demand in what he called its [9](__________)-growing market. Financial terms were not disclosed, but [10](a/an/the/x) two sources said the deal values the China unit at around [11](__________) (__________) dollars. That is far more than its valuation in 2017, when McDonald's agreed to sell [12](18/80)% of the business for up to [13](__________) (__________) dollars. Since then, the number of McDonald's stores in China has doubled to [14](__________), and the country has become its [15](__________) - (__________) market. It aims to have more than [16](__________) stores there within the next few years.

PHASE 3 *LISTENING & READING*

Synchro-Reading

1-37

Listen to the recording and read the following passage silently to understand what is said.

Starbucks, the world's leading coffee retailer, has long pursued a policy of expanding its business around the globe. The company was smart enough to understand that one single approach to business would not necessarily translate into success in every country and that it would be vital to take cultural differences into account.

Starbucks opened its first Japanese store in Ginza in 1996, and as of 2022 had more than 1,600. This remarkable degree of success was largely due to the company adapting its approach to suit the needs and tastes of Japanese consumers. One innovation was in the size of its cups. The company recognized that Japanese customers might prefer smaller measures, and so it introduced the "short" size specially for the Japanese market. It also understood that the US custom of drinking coffee while walking along the street was not popular in Japan. On the whole, Japanese customers prefer to drink their coffee in the store, and so Starbucks provides a lot of tables and chairs despite the relatively small size of its stores compared to the US.

Starbucks also understands that awareness of the changing seasons is an important aspect of Japanese culture. It has responded by providing seasonally themed offerings, such as sakura frappucino in spring and apple-themed drinks for fall, as well as special offerings at Halloween and Christmas. It is also aware of how much Japanese consumers love branded goods, and therefore offers exclusive products for a limited time, such as "lucky bags" (*fukubukuro*) at New Year.

Step 7 Vocabulary View

CD 1-38

Choose the definition or synonym for each of the following English words or phrases.

1. retailer	______	a. limited for a certain group or period of time
2. pursue	______	b. quantity, amount
3. vital	______	c. to follow
4. remarkable	______	d. a business that sells to the public
5. adapt	______	e. noticeable
6. measure	______	f. extremely important
7. provide	______	g. to make available
8. awareness	______	h. to make suitable
9. offerings	______	i. knowledge
10. exclusive	______	j. products; something provided for sale

Step 8 Reading Comprehension & Lexicogrammar: Word Choice

Choose (a)-(d) to complete each statement in a grammatically correct sentence so that it matches the content of the passage.

1. Starbucks has a policy of trying to expand its business ______ the world.
   a. up and around　b. around and about　c. all over　d. all throughout
2. Starbucks understood the importance of considering cultural ______ when opening stores in a new country.
   a. facts　b. factions　c. fictions　d. factors
3. Its success in Japan was ______ to its decision to adapt its approach to suit the Japanese market.
   a. due　b. because　c. according　d. resulting
4. In ______ to Americans, Japanese people do not often drink coffee while walking on the street.
   a. compare　b. contrast　c. difference　d. similarity
5. Starbucks offers seasonal goods because it knows Japanese people are ______ of the changing seasons.
   a. consequence　b. consulting　c. conscience　d. conscious

Step 9 Best Summary

Choose the best summary.

1. Starbucks has recently become the most popular coffee shop in Japan.
2. Starbucks has successfully adapted its approach to suit Japanese tastes.
3. Starbucks emphasizes US culture in the design of its stores.
4. Starbucks is most popular at special times such as Christmas and Halloween.
5. Starbucks has been more successful in Japan than in any other country.

Step 10 Free Writing & Interviewing

Write your answer for each of the following questions and then ask each other each of the following questions below.

A. Which is your favorite fast-food restaurant? Why?

....

....

....

1. How often do you go to fast-food restaurants?
2. What do you usually order? How much do you usually pay at one time?
3. Do you ever worry that eating too much junk food will affect your health?

B. Do you often go to Starbucks or similar coffee shops?

....

....

....

1. What kind of drink do you usually order in a coffee shop?
2. Do you prefer to go to a coffee shop alone or with friends?
3. Do you ever drink coffee or another type of drink while walking on the street?

Step 11 Template Essay Writing & Oral Presentation

Follow the template and write on the topic below and read it aloud in pairs or groups.

TOPIC: People should stop eating fast food for the sake of their health.

It is true that fast food is not a healthy choice. For example, ...

....

....

....

However, fast food is not entirely bad. ....

....

....

....

All in all, I believe that ....

....

....

....

Free Discussion

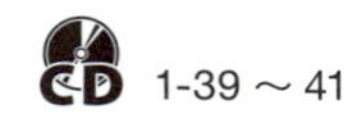
1-39 ～ 41

Listen to/read the model dialog and talk freely with your partner using the following question.

QUESTION: What do you usually order at a fast food restaurant?

Model Dialogs

Positive	Negative
A: What do you usually order at a fast food restaurant? **B:** I usually order a cheeseburger and a soda. **A:** How much do you usually pay at one time? **B:** Around 500 yen. **A:** Do you ever worry that eating too much junk food is bad for your health? **B:** I don't eat much, so I don't worry at all.	**A:** What do you usually order at a fast food restaurant? **B:** I rarely go to a fast food restaurant. **A:** How come? **B:** They aren't healthy. I don't like junk food. **A:** So, you're very health-conscious. **B:** Definitely. Health comes first. We must pay full attention to every meal we have every day.

Useful Patterns for Writing & Speaking from Unit 5

1	A has a policy of trying to B.	A は B をしようとする方針を持っている。
2	A has been more successful in B than in any other country.	A はどこの国よりも B で成功を収めてきています。
3	On the whole, A prefers to B.	概して A は B をするほうが好きです。
4	How often do you go to ～ ?	～へはどのくらいの頻度で行っていますか。
5	Do you ever worry that eating too much ～ will affect your health?	～の食べ過ぎが体に悪いと思うことはありますか。
6	Do you ever A while B-ing?	B をしながら A をすることはありますか。
7	It is true that ～ is not a healthy choice.	～が健康上良い選択ではないことは正しいです。
8	What do you usually order at ～ ?	～でふだんは何を注文しますか。
9	Do you ever worry that ～ is bad for your health?	～が体に良くないと思ったことはありませんか。
10	We must pay full attention to ～ .	～によく注意しなければなりません。

UNIT 6 Italian Cheese Makers Fight Fakes With Microchips

 1-42

産地表示 イタリアのチーズ生産者が偽造品撲滅に奮闘

Do you like cheese? In recent years, supermarkets in Japan have been selling a wide variety of cheeses imported from Europe, such as cheeses from France and Italy. The video focuses on an Italian cheese maker that uses advanced technology to counter false labeling. The essay gives a detailed description of food fraud. Let's learn about what is going on in the food industry and think about ways to protect ourselves against being tricked.

PHASE 1 *WARM UP*

Step 1 Photo Description

Look at the photo below and choose the sentence that best describes it.

1. The cheese wheels are being carried on the front of the forklift.
2. The forklift is operating without anyone driving it.
3. The cheese wheels have been cut into several pieces.
4. The cheese wheels are different from each other in size and shape.

Step 2 Vocabulary Preview

 1-43

Choose the Japanese equivalent for each of the following English words or phrases.

1. counterfeit	______	a. 着目させる (=to spotlight)
2. a grain of salt	______	b. ～に関連している (=be relevant to)
3. just to give a reference of	______	c. 円盤状の板
4. casein /kéisiːn/	______	d. カゼイン（タンパク質の一種）
5. wafer /wéifər/	______	e. 塩の粒
6. be embedded in	______	f. 追跡可能性
7. traceability	______	g. ～に埋め込まれている
8. be associated with	______	h. 偽造の (=fake; bogus; forged)
9. highlight	______	i. ～を例えて言うならば、～の目安として
10. via /váiə//víə/	______	j. ～を介して、～を通して (=through; by means [way] of)

PHASE 2 VIEWING & LISTENING

Step 3 Listening for Comprehension: Q&A

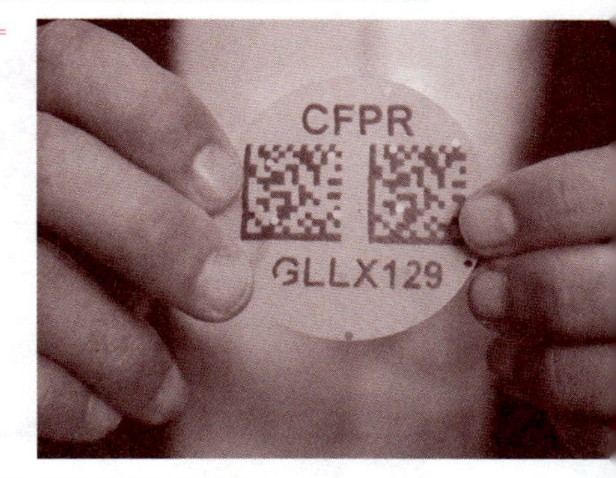

Watch the video and answer the following question.

(Time 01:47)

Q: How did the maker come to introduce the technology?

A: ....

....

Step 4 Listening for Comprehension: Multiple Choice

Watch the video again and choose the best answer for each of the following questions.

Q1: Compared with a grain of salt, how large is the chip?

A. Almost the same **B.** Slightly smaller **C.** Much smaller **D.** Not mentioned

Q2: Besides the location of the cheese, what can the chip trace?

A. The quality **B.** The quantity **C.** The price **D.** The owner

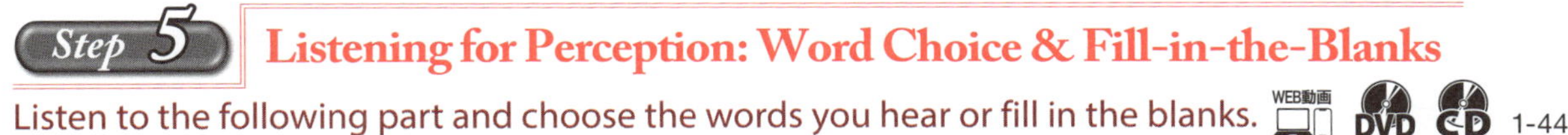

Step 5 Listening for Perception: Word Choice & Fill-in-the-Blanks

Listen to the following part and choose the words you hear or fill in the blanks. 1-44

Narrator: Italian producers of world-famous Parmigiano Reggiano are fighting against counterfeit products with [1](a/an/the/x) help of microchips attached to the crust of the cheese wheels.

Riccardo Deserti, General Manager of the Parmigiano Reggiano Consortium: We use [2](a/an/the/x) industrial technology to insert this chip, which is much smaller than a grain of salt, just to give a reference of the [3](size/sizes) of the chip, and this casein plate is made of very thin layers and is inserted in this sort of "wafer" and is [4](embedded/embedding) in the casein plate. 5

Narrator: The chip will contain traceability data including the place and date of production. An [5](__________)-pound wheel of Parmigiano Reggiano costs over $[6](__________) on Amazon.com. It's among the world's most counterfeited cheeses. 10

Riccardo Deserti, General Manager of the Parmigiano Reggiano Consortium: The total traceability not only of the cheeses but also of the kilos of [7](product /products) that are associated with the casein plate and in the future hopefully with the casein plate with this new chip technology, will improve the [8](ability/abilities) to control and also to be able to highlight and uncover counterfeiting problems. 15

Narrator: [9](__________) wheels of cheese can now be traced by consumers via the chip.

PHASE 3 *LISTENING & READING*

Synchro-Reading

1-45

Listen to the recording and read the following passage silently to understand what is said.

As consumers, we are often warned to be on our guard against food fraud. But what is it exactly? Put simply, food fraud is when dishonest people intentionally attempt to deceive customers about the content or quality of food products in order to benefit financially. The US food monitoring body, the Food and Drug Administration (FDA), 5 estimates that food fraud could be earning criminals around $40 billion a year.

Food fraud can take several forms. One is dilution, when a cheaper liquid is mixed in with a higher-quality one. Another is mislabeling, when false information is provided on the packaging. Yet another is secretly concealing the presence of unknown, low-quality food ingredients, which may be hazardous to our health.

10 Fortunately, there are now advanced technological tools available that can analyze food products to identify their ingredients. One such method is based on using infrared radiation. With this technique, an infrared beam is directed at a food item, which is placed in front of it. The results of this analysis make it possible to detect which substances are present in the food. This method has two great advantages: it is low cost 15 and it does not damage or destroy the food samples being used.

Another method is DNA-based detection, which is often used with meat or seafood products. If the manufacturer claims that product contains certain ingredients, DNA-based testing can either prove or disprove this. In addition, it can also identify other possibly harmful substances that are not mentioned in the list of ingredients.

Vocabulary View

1-46

Choose the definition or synonym for each of the following English words or phrases.

1. warn	______	a.	watching, checking
2. intentionally	______	b.	hiding
3. monitoring	______	c.	on purpose
4. estimate	______	d.	dangerous
5. dilution	______	e.	to find
6. concealing	______	f.	adding a weaker to a stronger liquid
7. hazardous	______	g.	to make aware of danger
8. infrared	______	h.	a warm and invisible light
9. beam	______	i.	to guess the size
10. detect	______	j.	a ray of light

Step 8 Reading Comprehension & Lexicogrammar: Word Choice

Choose (a)-(d) to complete each statement in a grammatically correct sentence so that it matches the content of the passage.

1. Some dishonest people commit food fraud with the ________ of benefiting financially.
   a. aim　b. reason　c. proposal　d. cause
2. False information is printed on labels in order to ________ consumers.
   a. mistake　b. misunderstand　c. mislead　d. mistrust
3. Substances ________ in food items can be detected using infrared radiation.
   a. contained　b. including　c. available　d. presence
4. Cheaper liquids can be used to ________ more expensive ones.
   a. dissolve　b. dilute　c. divert　d. dismiss
5. DNA-based testing is a way to ________ a manufacturer's claims about a product's ingredients.
   a. confirm　b. decide　c. guarantee　d. judge

Step 9 Best Summary

Choose the best summary.

1. An explanation of food fraud and how to deal with it
2. Suggestions for new ways to fight food fraud
3. Successful and unsuccessful attempts to fight food fraud
4. How technology has eliminated food fraud
5. Attempts by the US government to fight food fraud

Step 10 Free Writing & Interviewing

Write your answer for each of the following questions and then ask each other each of the following questions below.

A. How important do you think product traceability of food and drinks is for our health?

....

....

....

1. How much attention do you pay to what you buy?
2. Do you trust what is said on the label of the products you buy? Why or why not?
3. Have you ever bought fake products? When or how did you notice they were fake?

B. When buying food, is it a good idea spend more to get higher quality products?

....

....

....

1. How much do you usually spend on buying groceries per week
2. Do you buy mainly fresh food or processed food?
3. Do you usually cook your own meals or buy meals that have already been prepared?

Step 11 Template Essay Writing & Oral Presentation

Follow the template and write on the topic below and read it aloud in pairs or groups.

TOPIC: We should try to eat only fresh food and avoid all processed foods.

There is no doubt that fresh food is better for our health because ....

....

....

....

However, I think it is difficult to completely avoid processed foods because ....

....

....

....

To sum up, I believe that ....

....

....

....

Free Discussion

1-47 ～ 49

Listen to/read the model dialog and talk freely with your partner using the following question.

QUESTION: Do you think this method of protecting products with microchips will spread?

Model Dialogs

Positive	Negative
A: Do you think this method of protecting products with microchips will spread? **B:** Definitely. **A:** How come? **B:** The method explained in the video is quite innovative and appears to be less costly than any other countermeasure to prevent counterfeiting. **A:** In what other products do you think this microchip should be inserted? **B:** All kinds of food products. Not only processed food like cheese but also fresh food, say, meat or even seafood products if possible in the future.	**A:** Do you think this method of protecting products with microchips will spread? **B:** I'm not sure. **A:** Why? **B:** I agree that the technology has a lot of promise to make our lives better. But the expense of putting this type of chip into every product they make will be a financial burden for producers. **A:** But it's a way of protecting their brand. **B:** So, it's up to the maker to decide whether to use this technology if they believe that protecting their product is worth the cost.

Useful Patterns for Writing & Speaking from Unit 6

1	～ can take several forms.	～にはさまざまな形態があります。
2	How important do you think A is for B?	A は B にとってどのくらい大切であると思いますか。
3	How much attention do you pay to ～ ?	～にどのくらい注意していますか。
4	How much do you usually spend on buying ～ per week?	～を買うのにふだん毎週いくら払っていますか。
5	There is no doubt that A is better for B.	AのほうがBには良いことに疑いの余地はないです。
6	It is difficult to completely avoid ～ .	～を完全に防ぐことは困難です。
7	Do you think ～ will spread?	～は広まると思いますか。
8	I agree that ～ has a lot of promise to make our lives better.	～が我々の生活の向上にたいへん有望である点については同意します。
9	A will be a financial burden for B.	A は B にとって金銭的な負担になるでしょう。
10	It's up to A to decide whether to B.	B をするかどうかは A しだいです。

Customers Nap While Standing at a Tokyo "Sleep Cafe"

 1-50

睡眠 立ったまま寝る「睡眠カフェ」が東京にオープン

Do you sleep well every day? How do you sleep? On your back? On your side? On your stomach? The video presents a cafe in Tokyo that offers customers the chance to nap while standing up, like a giraffe, while the essay gives an account of the quality of sleep and different sleep customs. Try to describe your own sleep habits. Also, describe how you think your school or company should consider the importance of sleeping.

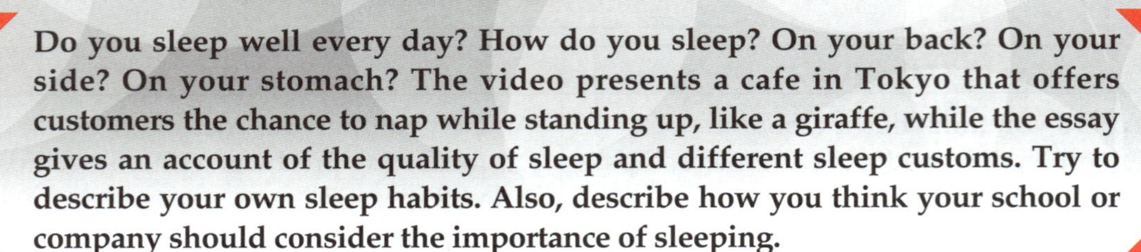

PHASE 1 *WARM UP*

Step 1 Photo Description

Look at the photo below and choose the sentence that best describes it.

1. Several pods are standing close together.
2. The middle pod is currently out of service.
3. There are no tables or chairs available in the room.
4. The pods all look alike in shape and design.

Step 2 Vocabulary Preview

 1-51

Choose the Japanese equivalent for each of the following English words or phrases.

1. nap	______	a. キリン
2. giraffe	______	b. 造り、構造、仕組み (=structure; system)
3. sleep while standing up	______	c. ～に重い負担をかける
4. knee	______	d. 短時間寝る、昼寝（うたた寝）する
5. surprisingly	______	e. 意外に、驚くほどに (=amazingly)
6. put much of a load on	______	f. 人気を博する (=to become popular)
7. setup	______	g. 横になる
8. lie down	______	h. ～に悪影響を与える
9. have a negative impact on	______	i. 膝、ひざ
10. take off	______	j. 立ったまま寝る

PHASE 2 *VIEWING & LISTENING*

Step 3 Listening for Comprehension: Q&A

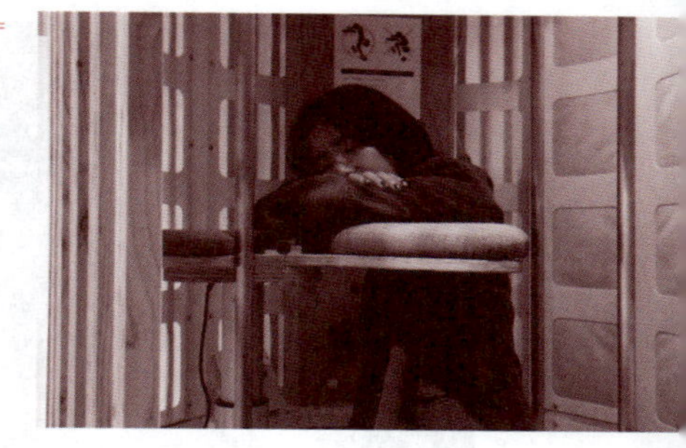

Watch the video and answer the following question.

(Time 01:28)

Q: How do the two customers evaluate the napping facilities?

A: ....

....

Listening for Comprehension: Multiple Choice

Watch the video again and choose the best answer for each of the following questions.

Q1: How many times had the second customer visited the cafe before?

A. Never **B.** Once **C.** Twice **D.** Several times

Q2: What is the problem of sleeping while lying down?

A. You could easily wake up.
B. You could sleep too long.
C. You could have a bad dream.
D. You could be late for work.

Step 5 Listening for Perception: Word Choice & Fill-in-the-Blanks

Listen to the following part and choose the words you hear or fill in the blanks. WEB動画 DVD CD 1-52

Narrator: If giraffes can sleep standing up, maybe you can too. A cafe in Tokyo lets customers [1](__________) while standing in these sleep pods.

Yoshihito Nohara, Giraffenap Manager: Every day, [2](a/an/the/x) giraffes sleep while standing up for about 20 minutes. Just like that, 20 minutes a day is just right for [3](a/an/the/x) nap too. That's why we [4](call/called) it the Giraffenap, because of [5](a/an/the/x) way giraffes rest.

Narrator: Roughly the size of a phone booth, the "Giraffepod" has enough space for one person.

Customer A: I thought standing up would be [6](tough/tougher) on my [7](knee/knees) but surprisingly it didn't really put much of a [8](load/road) on them. I felt like it was a really thoughtful setup.

Customer B: It was my [9](__________) time sleeping while standing up. My bodyweight was more [10](supported/supportive) than I expected.

Narrator: A half-hour snooze in a pod costs $5.60 at Nestle's "sleep cafe."

Jiro Takaoka, Manager, Nestle Japan: The thing is that if you [11](__________) (__________) to rest, you could [12](__________) sleep for one or two hours, which would have a negative impact on your sleep during [13](a/an/the/x) night. We've promoted the idea of sleeping while sitting but with this Giraffenap you can stand and sleep. It's great for a 20-minute nap, so we [14](order/ordered) it.

Narrator: The pod maker hopes it will take off in Japan, where OECD data shows people get [15](little/a little) sleep.

Synchro-Reading

Listen to the recording and read the following passage silently to understand what is said.

Medical experts tell us that getting enough good-quality sleep is crucial in maintaining our health. Most people would probably say that the ideal amount is between six and eight hours of unbroken sleep per night. But is this actually true?

There are countries in the world where sleeping in two segments is part of the culture. For example, in hot places such as Spain, Greece, and parts of South America, many people take a nap every afternoon. This custom is known as "siesta." In such places, it is not unusual for shops and other businesses to close for a few hours after lunch while people rest and escape from the afternoon heat.

The view of taking naps during the day seems to be changing. Napping is no longer seen as evidence of laziness or lack of energy. Rather, there is a focus on the many benefits it can have, including increased alertness, improved mood, reduced stress, and better learning and memory.

However, if you think that taking regular naps could be good for you, it is important to remember that the duration of the nap is very important. For most people, an ideal length is thought to be between 10 and 20 minutes. If the nap is any longer, it might take you some time to return to normal when you wake up. Also, napping for too long during the day could disrupt your sleep patterns at night, making you feel even more tired.

Sleep patterns vary from person to person, so napping may not be an ideal solution for everyone. If it does not work for you, just make sure to get six to eight hours of sleep at night.

Step 7 Vocabulary View

1-54

Choose the definition or synonym for each of the following English words or phrases.

1. crucial ______
2. unbroken ______
3. segment ______
4. nap ______
5. escape from ______
6. evidence ______
7. benefits ______
8. ideal ______
9. disrupt ______
10. solution ______

a. proof; verification
b. part
c. a means of solving a problem
d. desirable or perfect
e. to avoid
f. very important
g. continuous
h. short sleep
i. to disturb; to interrupt
j. good points; advantages

Step 8 Reading Comprehension & Lexicogrammar: Word Choice

Choose (a)-(d) to complete each statement in a grammatically correct sentence so that it matches the content of the passage.

1. Getting a good night's sleep is ______ to good overall health.
   a. indifferent b. indispensable c. intolerable d. inefficient

2. It is thought that people should ideally get ______ six hours of sleep each night.
   a. an average of b. a total of c. at least d. at most

3. The custom of siesta is ______ in certain hot parts of the world.
   a. beginning to disappear b. gaining popularity
   c. no longer practiced d. still part of life

4. There is increasing awareness that napping during the day can have ______.
   a. a variety of benefits b. serious consequences
   c. wide agreement d. strong criticism

5. It is ______ that napping during the day is good for everyone.
   a. generally accepted b. firmly rejected
   c. unfortunate d. not necessarily true

Step 9 Best Summary

Choose the best summary.

1. There is a general trend toward sleeping less at night and napping during the day.
2. Napping can have benefits, but it is usually regarded as a sign of laziness or bad health.
3. Napping is good for people who live in hot countries, but not so much for others.
4. A combination of sleeping well at night and napping during the day can be beneficial.
5. Taking naps is good because it allows us to sleep for fewer hours at night.

PHASE 4 ***WRITING & SPEAKING***

Step 10 Free Writing & Interviewing

Write your answer for each of the following questions and then ask each other each of the following questions below.

A. Do you think you sleep well and enough at night? If so, why? If not, why not?

....

....

....

1. How many hours do you sleep on average? Do you think you sleep enough?
2. How do you sleep? On your back? On your side? On your stomach?
3. Would you like to try the service at the "sleep cafe"? Why or why not?

B. Do you think you could work or study more effectively if you were able to take a nap during the day? Why or why not?

....

....

....

1. Do you often become sleepy while working at work or while sitting in a class?
2. Do you regularly take a nap?
3. Is there a facility for people to take a nap at your workplace or at your school?

Step 11 Template Essay Writing & Oral Presentation

Follow the template and write on the topic below and read it aloud in pairs or groups.

TOPIC: Companies should allow workers to nap during business hours.

There are certain points in favor of this argument. ....

....

....

....

However, there are also certain points against it. ....

....

....

....

My own feeling is that ....

....

....

....

Step 12 Free Discussion

CD 1-55 ～ 57

Listen to/read the model dialog and talk freely with your partner using the following question.

QUESTION: Do you sleep well?

Model Dialogs

Positive	Negative
A: Do you sleep well? **B:** Yes, I sleep well. **A:** How many hours do you usually sleep? **B:** At least 7 hours. **A:** Do you feel good when you wake up? **B:** I feel great every morning.	**A:** Do you sleep well? **B:** Not really. I'm sleepy all the time. **A:** Why? **B:** Well, I have many worries. **A:** Such as? **B:** Such as money and my future.

Useful Patterns for Writing & Speaking from Unit 7

1	A varies from person to person, so B may not be an ideal solution for everyone.	A は人によって違うので、B が誰にでも理想的な解決法ではないのかも知れません。
2	There is increasing awareness that ～ can have a variety of benefits.	～には様々な恩恵があるとの認識が高まっています。
3	There is a general trend toward ～ .	一般的に～をする傾向にあります。
4	A combination of A and B can be beneficial.	A と B を組み合わせると恩恵があります。
5	How many hours do you ～ on average?	あなたは平均して何時間～をしますか。
6	Do you think you could work or study more effectively if you were able to ～ ?	～をすることができたほうが仕事や勉強がよりはかどると思いますか。
7	Do you often become A while B-ing?	B をしている間に A になることはよくありますか。
8	Is there a facility for people to ～ at your workplace or at your school?	あなたの職場や学校に～ができる施設はありますか。
9	How many hours do you usually ～ ?	ふだん何時間～をしますか。
10	Do you feel good when you ～ ?	～をする時は気分が良いですか。

AI-Powered Facial Recognition System Reads Vital Signs

1-58

AI 診察 顔認識で脈拍数、酸素飽和度、呼吸数まで読み取る

Have you ever seen AI technology at hospitals? The video reports that AI face recognition technology has been developed in Japan. The device can estimate pulse rate, oxygen saturation, and respiratory rate without being worn on the body. How does it work? The essay describes various medical procedures that use AI. What does our future hold? Let your imagination run wild and express your predictions of AI uses in our future world.

PHASE 1 *WARM UP*

Step 1 Photo Description

Look at the photo below and choose the sentence that best describes it.

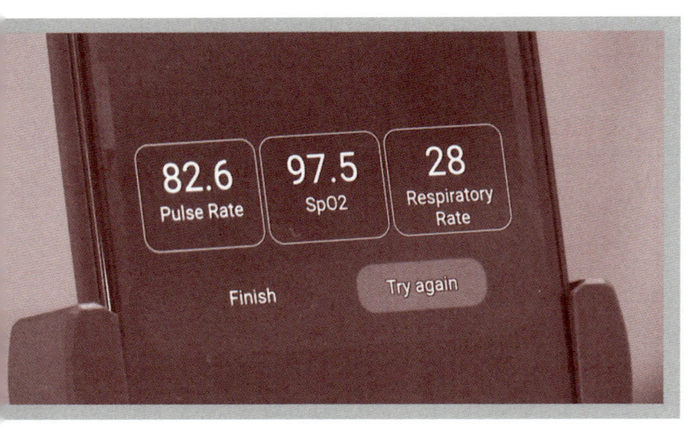

1. There are three readings displayed on the device.
2. There are two dial buttons located below the readings.
3. Indicators are written both in English and Japanese.
4. Explanations of the measurements are available on the panel.

Step 2 Vocabulary Preview

1-59

Choose the Japanese equivalent for each of the following English words or phrases.

1. vital signs ______
2. estimate ______
3. pulse rate ______
4. oxygen level ______
5. respiratory rate ______
6. rapidly ______
7. elder ______
8. device ______
9. health status ______
10. exhibit ______

a. 高齢者 (=senior citizen)
b. 脈拍数 (=the number of times the heart beats per minute)
c. 健康状態
d. 急速に (=quickly; swiftly; fast)
e. 呼吸数
f. 見せる、展示（提示）する (=to show)
g. 酸素レベル、酸素飽和度
h. 推定（評価、判断）する (=to roughly calculate)
i. バイタル数値
j. 装置 (=tool; gadget)

PHASE 2 *VIEWING & LISTENING*

Step 3 Listening for Comprehension: Q&A

Watch the video and answer the following question.  (Time 01:01)

Q: What is unique about this invention?

A: ....

....

Listening for Comprehension: Multiple Choice

Watch the video again and choose the best answer for each of the following questions.

Q1: What motivated the company to develop this device?

A. Low birthrate **B.** Rapidly aging population **C.** Inflation **D.** Not mentioned

Q2: What is thought to be difficult for elderly people to wear?

A. Oxygen mask **B.** Smart watch **C.** Ventilator **D.** Not mentioned

Listening for Perception: Word Choice & Fill-in-the-Blanks

Listen to the following part and choose the words you hear or fill in the blanks. WEB動画 DVD CD 1-60

Narrator: Hitoshi Imaoka, [1](a/an/the/x) fellow with IT and network technologies company NEC, has unveiled a new system that combines AI with [2](a/an/the/x) facial recognition technology to take vital signs in elderly individuals.

Hitoshi Imaoka: This is [3](a/an/the/x) display that estimates vital information from [4](a/an/the/x) face. It can measure three things, pulse rate, oxygen level and respiratory rate from the face. The [5](____________) point of this system is that it can measure within [6](____________) seconds. In recent years, the population of the world has been [7](aged/aging) rapidly and the number of [8](elder/elderly) people is increasing. I think it's probably difficult for an [9](elder/elderly) to wear a device like a smart watch. So we [10](want/wanted) to create a system that can examine people's health status just by [11](a/an/the/x) look of their faces, and that's [12](how/why) we are exhibiting it here.

Narrator: Hitoshi Imaoka said they hope to add other measurements like stress [13](level/levels) and focus ability as they continue to develop the system.

PHASE 3 LISTENING & READING

Step 6 Synchro-Reading

1-61

Listen to the recording and read the following passage silently to understand what is said.

As artificial intelligence (AI) technology continues to advance rapidly, it is transforming almost every sphere of human activity, and healthcare is no exception. AI's key strength is its ability to analyze huge amounts of data more quickly and accurately than even the most gifted and experienced human specialists. This has the potential to revolutionize the way medicine is practiced and lead to vastly improved outcomes for patients.

As an example, in 2015, IBM developed an AI tool called Watson, which analyzes enormous amounts of data with the specific aim of diagnosing and treating cancer patients. Watson can analyze not only information related to patients, such as medical history, genetic information, and test results, but also thousands of research articles and results of clinical trials. This can save doctors a lot of time, a crucial element in treating cancer patients effectively.

Medical imaging is another field in which AI's abilities can be used to great advantage. It takes a long time for human specialists to analyze CT scans or MRI images in order to make an accurate diagnosis. AI, on the other hand, can complete the task in seconds, often with a higher level of accuracy. This means that doctors are now able to quickly distinguish between serious and non-serious cases, allowing them to focus on patients who need more extensive care.

AI is also having a big impact in making medical treatment more personal. Using AI tools that can analyze someone's medical history, genetic makeup, and lifestyle, doctors can build up a detailed picture of an individual. This enables them to tailor treatments effectively to each patient rather than base treatments on impersonal, standardized rules.

Step 7 Vocabulary View

1-62

Choose the definition or synonym for each of the following English words or phrases.

1. advance	______	a. result
2. sphere	______	b. to find the cause of a problem
3. gifted	______	c. field
4. outcome	______	d. true and precise
5. diagnose	______	e. with a wide range
6. accurate	______	f. to move forward
7. distinguish	______	g. general, not targeting a particular individual
8. extensive	______	h. to fit, to suit
9. tailor	______	i. to decide how two things are different
10. impersonal	______	j. talented

Step 8 Reading Comprehension & Lexicogrammar: Word Choice

Choose (a)-(d) to complete each statement in a grammatically correct sentence so that it matches the content of the passage.

1. AI will bring ______ great changes in the field of medical care.
   a. along　b. back　c. about　d. through

2. AI promises to bring ______ changes to the way medicine is currently practiced.
   a. revolutionary　b. revolution　c. revolting　d. revolutionized

3. Timely ______ is an extremely important part of treating cancer patients.
   a. operation　b. therapy　c. medication　d. diagnosis

4. Doctors need to make an accurate ______ between cases that are serious and those that are not.
   a. distinguish　b. distinctive　c. distinction　d. distinct

5. It is important for doctors to ______ up a detailed profile of individual patients.
   a. build　b. grow　c. make　d. analyze

Step 9 Best Summary

Choose the best summary.

1. As AI advances, we will need fewer doctors to treat patients.
2. AI is mainly being used in the field of cancer treatment.
3. AI led to the invention of MRI and CT scanning technology.
4. AI is making medical treatment both more effective and more personal.
5. AI is helping scientists to write more and better research papers.

Step 10 Free Writing & Interviewing

Write your answer for each of the following questions and then ask each other each of the following questions below.

A. What do you think about this new system to read our vital information?

....

....

....

1. Do you think this system can be trusted?
2. To what extent do you think this device should be used at hospitals?
3. Do you think this new system will replace traditional ones at hospitals?

B. Are you mostly satisfied with the medical care you receive from doctors and dentists?

....

....

....

1. Do you think AI will improve medical and dental care for you personally?
2. How important is it for doctors to know personal information about a patient, such as lifestyle and family history?
3. Should we take more personal responsibility for our own health rather than rely on doctors?

Step 11 Template Essay Writing & Oral Presentation

Follow the template and write on the topic below and read it aloud in pairs or groups.

TOPIC: In the field of healthcare, AI will bring great benefits to everyone.

It is true that AI will certainly improve some types of medical care. For example,

....

....

....

However, I wonder if these benefits will be shared by everyone. ....

....

....

....

In conclusion, I can say that ....

....

....

....

Step 12 Free Discussion

1-63 ～ 65

Listen to/read the model dialog and talk freely with your partner using the following question.

QUESTION: How would you evaluate this AI-powered facial recognition system that can read vital signs?

Model Dialogs

Positive	Negative
A: How would you evaluate this AI-powered facial recognition system that can read vital signs? **B:** It's amazing. Wonderful! **A:** Do you think this invention will benefit us all? **B:** Definitely. It would be great if we could install the system in our smartphones. **A:** I totally agree. What else do you think an AI facial recognition system will be able to do in the future? **B:** I would say that an AI facial recognition system can tell what people are thinking or feeling.	**A:** How would you evaluate this AI powered facial recognition system that can read vital signs? **B:** To be honest. I don't trust it. **A:** How so? **B:** I can hardly believe that the new system can collect such vital data just by looking. The report doesn't mention the accuracy of measurements at all, compared to ordinary methods. **A:** So, there is no guarantee that the device can provide accurate information about our health. **B:** Exactly. I would like to get more details.

Useful Patterns for Writing & Speaking from Unit 8

1	A's key strength is its ability to B.	A の主な強みは B をする能力です。
2	How important is it for A to B?	A が B をすることはどのくらい大切なことですか。
3	How would you evaluate ～ ?	～をあなたならどのように評価しますか。
4	Do you think ～ will benefit us all?	～は我々全員に恩恵をもたらすと思いますか。
5	It would be great if we could ～ .	～をすることができれば素晴らしいことです。
6	What else do you think ～ will be able to do in the future?	～が将来できることは他に何があると思いますか。
7	I can hardly believe that ～ .	～であるとは到底考えられません。
8	I would say that ～ .	～であるということでしょう。
9	It is hard for me to believe that ～ .	～であるということは信じがたいです。
10	There is no guarantee that ～ .	～であるという保証はありません。

UNIT 9

Inside Gym Classes in the Metaverse

 2-01

筋トレ メタバースの仮想空間で行う筋トレ

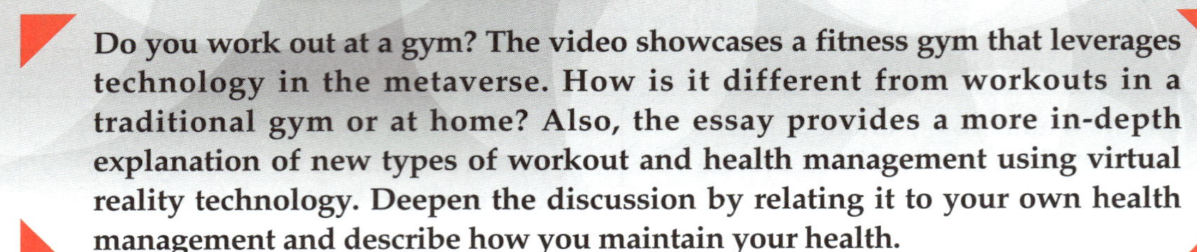

Do you work out at a gym? The video showcases a fitness gym that leverages technology in the metaverse. How is it different from workouts in a traditional gym or at home? Also, the essay provides a more in-depth explanation of new types of workout and health management using virtual reality technology. Deepen the discussion by relating it to your own health management and describe how you maintain your health.

PHASE 1 *WARM UP*

Step 1 Photo Description

Look at the photo below and choose the sentence that best describes it.

1. The woman at the front is wearing armbands.
2. Two people are watching a woman exercise on a screen.
3. All the people are dressed in sportswear.
4. The three people are exercising together.

Step 2 Vocabulary Preview

 2-02

Choose the Japanese equivalent for each of the following English words or phrases.

1. metaverse ______
2. startup ______
3. patented ______
4. virtual reality ______
5. fitness workouts ______
6. electrical impulse ______
7. interactive resistance ______
8. load ______
9. noticeable ______
10. bulky ______

a. 特許取得済みの
b. 新規企業 (=a company that has just been started)
c. 電気刺激
d. 仮想現実
e. インタラクティブな抵抗（力）、相互作用型の抵抗（力）
f. 筋トレ (=muscle training)
g. 顕著な (=conspicuous)
h. メタバース
i. 大きくて扱いにくい、かさばる
j. 負荷、重量、重さ (=weight)

PHASE 2 *VIEWING & LISTENING*

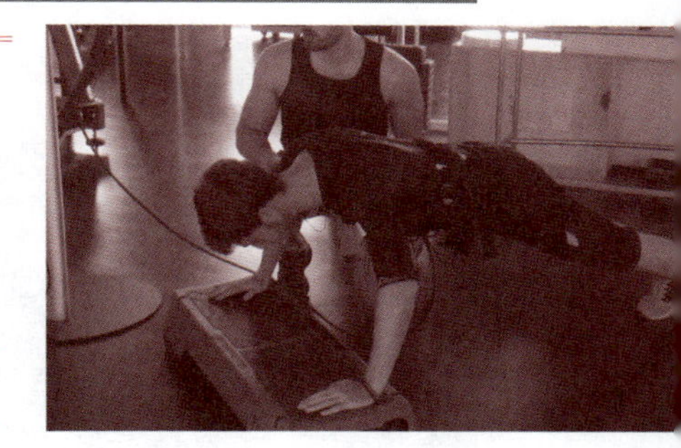

Step 3 Listening for Comprehension: Q&A

Watch the video and answer the following question.

(Time 01:47)

Q: How does this technology work?

A: ....

....

Step 4 Listening for Comprehension: Multiple Choice

Watch the video again and choose the best answer for each of the following questions.

Q1: Where is this tech company based?

A. The United States **B.** Canada **C.** Britain **D.** Australia

Q2: How often should EMS be used to gain noticeable benefits?

A. Every hour **B.** Every day **C.** Every two days **D.** Every three days

Step 5 Listening for Perception: Word Choice & Fill-in-the-Blanks

Listen to the following part and choose the words you hear or fill in the blanks.

2-03

Narrator: This is what [1](a/an/the/x) gym class looks like in the metaverse. [2](__________) - (__________) tech startup Valkyrie Industries is using its [3](patent/patented/patenting) wearable technology to allow users to take part in virtual reality fitness workouts. With [4](a/an/the/x) headset, two armbands and handheld devices, the setup can make your [5](brain/brains) think you are actually lifting weights. Kourosh Atefipour is the co-founder and CEO of the company. 5

Kourosh Atefipour: So we use electro-muscular stimulation, EMS for short, which fundamentally interacts with your [6](muscle/muscles) to create that same electrical impulse that your brain perceives when you're holding a cup, a mug, a water bottle, or a dumbbell and we're delivering that artificially [7](through/to) our wearables. 10

Narrator: Valkyrie's EIR armbands can provide unprecedented interactive resistance for the arm [8](muscle/muscles). The intensity changes depending on how strongly you pull a virtual elastic band, how quickly you lift a virtual dumbbell, or how hard you hit a virtual punching bag.

Kourosh Atefipour: So, [9](a/an/the/x) feeling you get out of these is resistance, load, fatigue and weight, up to a certain level, but it's designed more for strengthening, toning and conditioning. 15

Narrator: Electro-muscle stimulation has been used in sports medicine for decades, primarily to relieve muscle [10](pain/pains) and facilitate muscle training. Valkyrie says as little as [11](__________) minutes every two days can bring [12](__________) benefits without the [13](__________) equipment of other home setups. The company is [14](partnered/partnering) with global sports brand ASICS to develop its EIR virtual fitness training [15](platform/platforms). 20

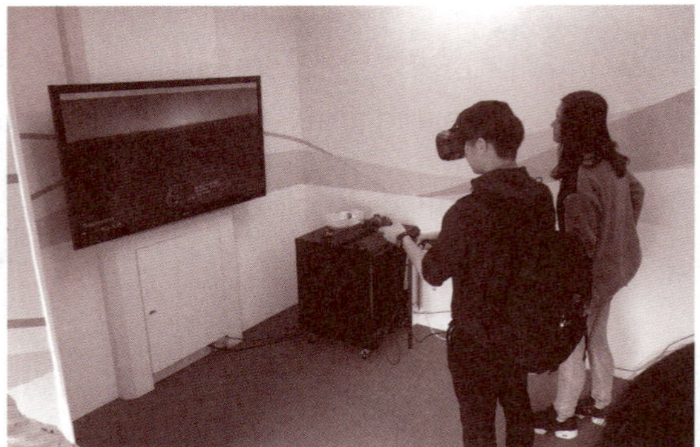

Synchro-Reading

2-04

Listen to the recording and read the following passage silently to understand what is said.

Health experts are constantly reminding us of the importance of physical activity if we wish to live a long and healthy life. Some people, however, are not motivated by the idea of exercising at a gym. Among other things, they may find it difficult to understand how to use the equipment properly or dislike the monotony of running on a treadmill.

5 One development that has the potential to completely change our relationship to exercise is the use of virtual reality (VR), which can combine working out with the fun and excitement of gaming. For a more stimulating exercise experience, all we need to do is to put on a VR headset, download a fitness app, and find enough space in our home to move around. We will then find ourselves completely immersed in a new digital 10 environment, maybe on a mountaintop, in the middle of a forest, or in a fantasy land. Rather than repetitively lifting weights, exercises could include killing virtual dragons, sword fighting, or dodging attacks by enemies. And to avoid becoming bored, we could choose new settings and different activities for each exercise session. What is more, just as in a game, the app can provide us with further incentives to increase motivation, such as 15 scores, targets, and the chance to rise through different levels.

Also, rather than exercising alone, many people find it more fun to do it with friends. Those who choose conventional gyms have found that an effective way to encourage regular workouts is to be part of a group of so-called "gym buddies." One advantage of VR fitness apps is that they are often interactive, enabling us to include our friends in 20 multiplayer sessions.

Step 7 Vocabulary View

2-05

Choose the definition or synonym for each of the following English words or phrases.

1. constantly	________	a. to avoid
2. monotony	________	b. exciting
3. potential	________	c. more
4. stimulating	________	d. happening again and again
5. immersed	________	e. possibility
6. repetitively	________	f. continually; never ending; endlessly
7. dodge	________	g. boredom; lack of variety or excitement
8. further	________	h. ordinary, familiar
9. incentive	________	i. completely surrounded by
10. conventional	________	j. promise of a reward

Step 8 Reading Comprehension & Lexicogrammar: Word Choice

Choose (a)-(d) to complete each statement in a grammatically correct sentence so that it matches the content of the passage.

1. Health experts stress the importance of being physically ________ if we want to stay healthy.
   a. activity   b. active   c. action   d. activate

2. Many people are ________ going to the gym by boring exercises such as running on a treadmill.
   a. called off   b. broken off   c. put off   d. taken off

3. Virtual environments can ________ the monotony of regular exercise into a kind of adventure.
   a. deliver   b. achieve   c. create   d. transform

4. VR exercise apps give us the ________ to choose a variety of virtual settings.
   a. situation   b. method   c. opportunity   d. condition

5. Many people would ________ exercise with friends than exercise alone.
   a. rather   b. better   c. more   d. prefer

Step 9 Best Summary

Choose the best summary.

1. More people are now using VR to exercise than attending gyms.
2. VR can create stimulating environments that encourage people to exercise.
3. More people would use VR exercise apps if they were cheaper.
4. VR exercise apps mainly appeal to people who like to exercise with friends.
5. VR exercise apps are chiefly used by fans of video games.

Step 10 Free Writing & Interviewing

Write your answer for each of the following questions and then ask each other each of the following questions below.

A. How much attention do you pay to your health?

....

....

....

1. Do you work out regularly?
2. Do you go to a gym? If so, how often do you go there?
3. Would you like to use this exercise method?

B. Do you need to have some form of entertainment while you exercise?

....

....

....

1. Do you ever listen to music through headphones while exercising?
2. What kind of music do you think is the best to listen to while exercising?
3. Do you think you would exercise more if you had "gym buddies"?

Step 11 Template Essay Writing & Oral Presentation

Follow the template and write on the topic below and read it aloud in pairs or groups.

TOPIC: How do you keep fit?

There are many ways to keep fit, including ....

....

....

....

Personally speaking, I prefer ....

....

....

....

However, everyone is different, and so ....

....

....

....

Step 12 Free Discussion

2-06 ~ 08

Listen to/read the model dialog and talk freely with your partner using the following question.

QUESTION: Do you think this business will be successful in Japan?

Model Dialogs

Positive	Negative
A: Do you think this business will be successful in Japan? **B:** Yes, this method is very attractive and practical. **A:** How so? **B:** It doesn't require much space and it looks enjoyable. **A:** I see. How is it different from traditional methods? **B:** I think this method will keep us motivated longer.	**A:** Do you think this business will be successful in Japan? **B:** I'm afraid not. **A:** How come? **B:** The device could be successful but it wouldn't be good for gym operators. **A:** What do you mean? **B:** You don't need to go to a gym to do this metaverse fitness training. You can do it at home.

Useful Patterns for Writing & Speaking from Unit 9

1	A changes depending on B.	A は B によって変わります。
2	All we need to do is to ～ .	～をするだけで良いです。
3	A stresses the importance of being B.	A は B であることの大切さを力説しています。
4	How is A different from B?	A は B とどう違いますか。
5	What kind of A do you think is the best to B?	B をするためにはどのような A が一番良いと思いますか。
6	Do you think you would A if you had B?	仮に B があればあなたは A をすると思いますか。
7	There are many ways to ～ .	～するには多くの方法があります。
8	Do you think A will be successful in B?	A は B で成功すると思いますか。
9	How is A different from B?	A は B とどう違うのですか。
10	You don't need to A to B.	B をするために A をする必要はありません。

UNIT 10 Multi-Tasking Robot Hopes to Revolutionize City Living

 2-09

ロボット 多機能ロボットで都市生活に大変革が起きるか

What do you imagine when you hear the word "robot"? Robots are becoming a part of the modern landscape, and we see a report that multifunctional robots have been developed in Germany and are already being used in a variety of scenarios. The essay illustrates the functions and uses of AI robots developed by a US company. Express your point of view on some other ways in which robots can benefit us and how they will affect our future.

PHASE 1 *WARM UP*

Step 1 Photo Description

Look at the photo below and choose the sentence that best describes it.

© EDAG Group

1. The car is driving alongside the plane.
2. The car has features that an ordinary car does not have.
3. The plane is about to land on the runway.
4. We can see both of the plane's engines clearly.

Step 2 Vocabulary Preview

 2-10

Choose the Japanese equivalent for each of the following English words or phrases.

1. revolutionize ______
2. mow one's lawn ______
3. autonomous ______
4. operational ______
5. municipal ______
6. chore ______
7. hydrogen ______
8. differentiate ______
9. bot ______
10. tarmac ______

a. 自律的な (=able to operate independently)
b. 雑用、日課、日常業務 (=a routine task)
c. 革命を起こす、大変革をもたらす (=to change radically)
d. 稼働可能な (=working)
e. ロボット (=robot)
f. 区別する (=to distinguish)
g. 市の、自治体の、地方自治の
h. 芝刈りをする
i. 水素
j. （空港の）駐機場

PHASE 2 *VIEWING & LISTENING*

Step 3 Listening for Comprehension: Q&A

Watch the video and answer the following question.

(Time 01:20)

Q: What does the CityBot do?

A: ....

....

Step 4 Listening for Comprehension: Multiple Choice

Watch the video again and choose the best answer for each of the following questions.

Q1: How long can the robot car keep working?

A. Several hours a day **B.** Half a day **C.** 24 hours **D.** It depends on the kind of work.

Q2: Who is in charge of cleaning streets?

A. The central government **B.** The local government **C.** Local residents **D.** Anyone

Step 5 Listening for Perception: Word Choice & Fill-in-the-Blanks

Listen to the following part and choose the words you hear or fill in the blanks. WEB動画 DVD CD 2-11

Narrator: This robot car might collect your trash and [1](   ) (   ) (   ) one day. Autonomous and [2](emission/emissions) -free, the CityBot aims to [3](   ) city living.

Johannes Brackmann: It's [4](   ) around the clock with [5](a/an/the/x) different modules which can be attached to it. During the day it [6](will/would) transport people and goods and in the evenings and during the night, it [7](will/would) take care of [8](   ) (   ) such as lawn mowing, emptying trash cans, shoveling snow, cleaning streets or watering trees.

Narrator: The robot is powered by electricity or [9](   ). AI and machine learning enable it to differentiate and separate objects, such as garbage.

Johannes Brackmann: Highly [10](automated/automatic) also means there are [11](automated/automatic) booking procedures such as emptying a paper basket [12](when/where) a sensor detects the paper. The bot [13](will/would) show up automatically and empty the paper basket and that's also [14](when/where) the paper basket [15](will/would) pay money for its emptying.

Narrator: The company plans to deploy CityBots to airports to guide planes on the tarmac and handle [16](baggage/luggage).

 Synchro-Reading  2-12

Listen to the recording and read the following passage silently to understand what is said.

Recently there have been countless news stories about how the incredible power of AI will transform the world of work in sophisticated fields such as data analysis, computer programming, translation, and self-driving vehicles. But it is important to remember that AI also has some everyday uses that can make our domestic lives much more convenient.

A startup company based in New York has developed an AI-powered robot that will take over some of the most burdensome chores for people who live in houses: cutting grass, collecting fallen leaves, and clearing snow. The robot, named Kobi, navigates with the help of a camera, an ultrasound sensor, and two beacons that are placed in the yard. But before it can operate independently, owners must carry out some safety measures. To do this, they have to manually wheel Kobi around the yard so that it can learn where the edges of the lawn are and avoid obstacles such as trees, bushes, and mailboxes. However, the manufacturer admits that Kobi cannot deal with every type of terrain. It says that while the robot can handle inclines of up to 40 percent, it may get stuck in deep holes.

Aside from taking over yard work duty, thereby giving people more free time, Kobi has other important benefits. For one thing, it can cut wastage. It is estimated that people spill more than 60 million liters of fuel every year when refueling lawn equipment. For another, its ability to shovel snow can protect people with heart problems. The combination of strenuous effort and cold weather poses an increased risk of heart attacks.

Step 7 Vocabulary View

2-13

Choose the definition or synonym for each of the following English words or phrases.

1. sophisticated	______	a. physical features of a piece of land
2. domestic	______	b. carefully tended grass
3. chore	______	c. high level, complicated
4. navigate	______	d. a device that sends signals
5. beacon	______	e. unable to move
6. lawn	______	f. to direct the way that a vehicle will travel
7. terrain	______	g. requiring physical effort
8. incline	______	h. relating to the home
9. stuck	______	i. an unpleasant or boring regular task
10. strenuous	______	j. hill or slope

Step 8 Reading Comprehension & Lexicogrammar: Word Choice

Choose (a)-(d) to complete each statement in a grammatically correct sentence so that it matches the content of the passage.

1. AI-powered devices are not ______ to the world of work.
   a. eliminated b. withdrawn c. restricted d. prevented

2. ______ devices such as a camera and sensors, Kobi can navigate effectively.
   a. Thanks to b. For the sake of c. As regards d. Concerned with

3. Kobi can ______ several common household chores that people find burdensome.
   a. sort out b. decide between c. hand over d. deal with

4. Refueling lawn equipment can be a very ______ activity.
   a. wasted b. wasting c. wasteful d. wastage

5. People with weak hearts ______ the risk of having a heart attack while doing yard work.
   a. run b. challenge c. take d. put

Step 9 Best Summary

Choose the best summary.

1. Kobi is one of many AI-powered robots that can help with domestic chores.
2. There is little demand for AI devices that can be used in the home.
3. An AI-powered robot that can help with domestic chores is now available.
4. The main purpose of Kobi is to prevent people from having heart attacks.
5. Kobi is a robot that can be used both inside and outside the house.

PHASE 4 *WRITING & SPEAKING*

Step 10 Free Writing & Interviewing

Write your answer for each of the following questions and then ask each other each of the following questions below.

A. Do you think robots will bring us a brighter future? Why or why not?

....

....

....

1. In what areas do you think robots can play significant roles? Why?
2. Do you think robots will take away every job from humans in the future?
3. What do you think will happen if humans continue to depend on robots?

B. What are some necessary but unpleasant chores that AI could make easier?

....

....

....

1. Which domestic chores do you dislike most?
2. What kind of AI device would help you most in your house or apartment?
3. What kind of AI technology do you use in daily life?

Step 11 Template Essay Writing & Oral Presentation

Follow the template and write on the topic below and read it aloud in pairs or groups.

TOPIC: Will AI make life better for us?

There is no doubt that AI will make some aspects of our life much easier. ....

....

....

....

On the other hand, we should not let AI take over every human task. ....

....

....

....

My own view of AI is that ....

....

....

....

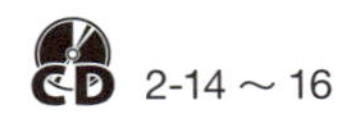

Step 12 Free Discussion

CD 2-14 ~ 16

Listen to/read the model dialog and talk freely with your partner using the following question.

QUESTION: Do you think robots will benefit us even more in the future?

Model Dialogs

Positive	Negative
A: Do you think robots will benefit us even more in the future? **B:** Definitely. They will solve problems of labor shortage. **A:** In what areas? **B:** War and medicine. **A:** How? **B:** Flying robots like military drones will save pilots' lives and robot surgeons will be able to operate on more patients more quickly than human doctors.	**A:** Do you think robots will benefit us even more in the future? **B:** I doubt it. **A:** Why? **B:** We will realize that we depend too much on robots or other technology such as AI and will make a wise decision to continue to be humans. **A:** What do you mean? **B:** We should just do whatever we need to do with our own hands.

Useful Patterns for Writing & Speaking from Unit 10

1	Recently there have been countless news stories about ～ .	最近～に関するニュースが数え切れないほどあります。
2	People with A run the risk of B.	A を抱える人は B をする危険性があります。
3	There is little demand for ～ .	～に対する需要はほとんどありません。
4	The main purpose of A is to prevent people from B.	A の主な目的は人が B をするのを防ぐことです。
5	In what areas do you think ～ can play significant roles?	～はどの分野で重要な役割を果たすと思いますか。
6	What do you think will happen if humans continue to ～ ?	人間が～をし続ければ何が起きると思いますか。
7	Which ～ do you dislike most?	どの～が一番嫌いですか。
8	What kind of ～ do you use in daily life?	あなたは日常生活でどのような～を使っていますか。
9	Do you think ～ will benefit us even more in the future?	～は将来さらに我々に恩恵をもたらすと思いますか。
10	We should just do whatever we need to ～ .	我々は～をするのに必要なことは何でもすべきです。

Solar-Powered Cars Race Through Australian Outback

太陽光電池 オーストラリアの奥地でソーラーカーレース開催

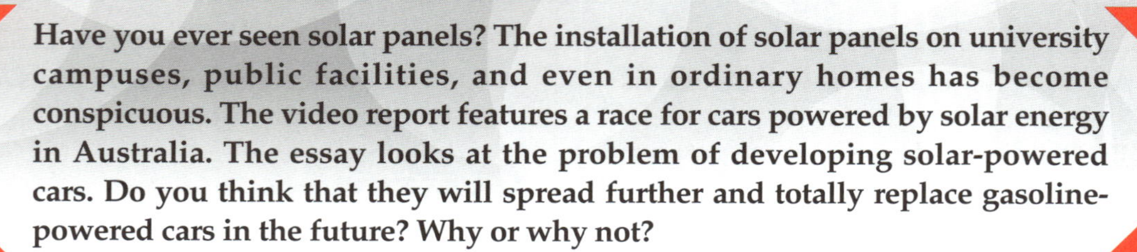

Have you ever seen solar panels? The installation of solar panels on university campuses, public facilities, and even in ordinary homes has become conspicuous. The video report features a race for cars powered by solar energy in Australia. The essay looks at the problem of developing solar-powered cars. Do you think that they will spread further and totally replace gasoline-powered cars in the future? Why or why not?

PHASE 1 *WARM UP*

Step 1 Photo Description

Look at the photo below and choose the sentence that best describes it.

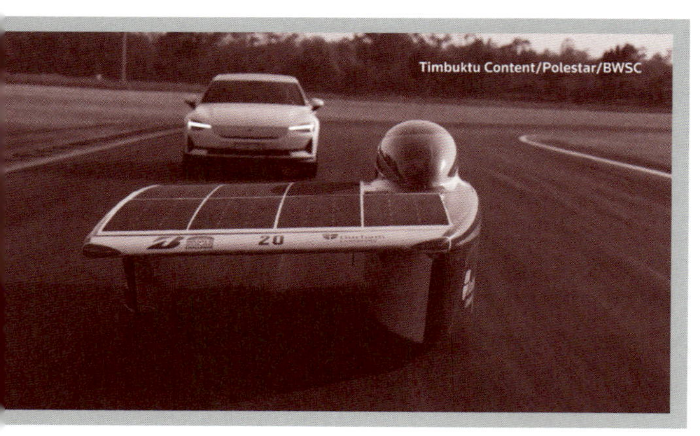

1. The solar car is attached to the regular car behind it.
2. The two vehicles are driving alongside each other.
3. The two vehicles are parked at the side of the road.
4. The car in front is covered with solar panels on the top.

Step 2 Vocabulary Preview

Choose the Japanese equivalent for each of the following English words or phrases.

1. outback	______	a. 気づく (=become aware of)
2. innovation	______	b. 〜から構成される (=to be composed of)
3. efficiency	______	c. 効率
4. comprised of	______	d. 見積もり (=rough calculation)
5. logistics	______	f. 奥地 (=a remote inland district)
6. estimate	______	g. 明らかに、明白に (=clearly; obviously)
7. roughly	______	h. 革新、改革 (=a new idea or method)
8. obviously	______	e. 通気口、空気穴
9. air vent	______	i. 兵站(へいたん)(業務) (=the handling of the details of an operation)
10. notice	______	j. おおよそ、約 (= about; approximately)

PHASE 2 *VIEWING & LISTENING*

Step 3 Listening for Comprehension: Q&A

Watch the video and answer the following question.  (Time 01:09)

Q: What kind of people mostly participate in this race?

A: ....

....

 Step 4 Listening for Comprehension: Multiple Choice 

Watch the video again and choose the best answer for each of the following questions.

Q1: Where is the goal of the solar car race?

A. Durham **B.** Darwin **C.** Adelaide **D.** Not mentioned

Q2: What is installed in the woman's car?

A. Air conditioning **B.** An air cushion **C.** An air vent **D.** Not mentioned

 Step 5 Listening for Perception: Word Choice & Fill-in-the-Blanks

Listen to the following part and choose the words you hear or fill in the blanks. WEB動画   2-19

Narrator: These electric cars are racing against each other across the Australian [1](**outback/outbacks**) powered only by the energy of the sun. The Bridgestone World Solar Challenge brings together teams from across the world to take part in an over [2](__________)-mile-long race and push the limits of technological innovation.

Peake-Jones, Head of electrical, Durham University Solar Car: So we're driving forward efficient car design and we're also driving forward solar technology and electrical [3](**efficiency/efficiencies**) in general. 5

Narrator: The challenge starts in Darwin and finishes in Adelaide about five days later, with the cars expected to cover the course in [4](__________) hours. Teams are usually comprised of [5](__________) (__________) who engineer and build the [6](**vehicle/vehicles**). 10 One of the participating teams are from Durham University. Catherine Flanders is the head of logistics for the team.

Catherine Flanders: So we don't have any air conditioning in our car. So the estimate is that our car is roughly [7](__________) degrees warmer than the outside air temperature, which puts the inside of the car about [8](__________) degrees-C, 15 obviously it's very warm. We have an air vent that keeps you cool, but you're so [9](**focused/focusing**) on what you're doing that you don't really notice [10](**a/an/the/x**) heat until you're out of it again.

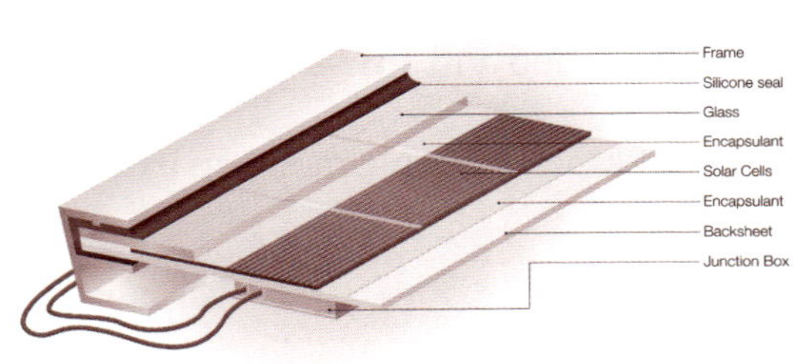

Step 6 Synchro-Reading

2-20

Listen to the recording and read the following passage silently to understand what is said.

The cars that take part in the World Solar Challenge look more like cars that you would see in a science-fiction movie than vehicles that you might see driving along city streets. The purpose of their large horizontal surfaces is to carry as many solar cells as possible to capture enough energy from the sun to power the cars over long distances.

The challenge of collecting enough sunlight is just one of several practical problems that solar-powered cars face. These problems make it difficult for such cars to compete in the marketplace with regular gasoline-powered cars or electric vehicles that run on lithium batteries. In order to acquire sufficient power, solar cars need constant exposure to sunlight. This would obviously be a problem at night or in places that regularly experience cloudy weather.

Not only do solar-powered cars need to carry a lot of solar cells, they also need to be equipped with batteries to store power. Both of these factors increase the weight of the car, meaning that it requires more power, and having passengers in addition to the driver would increase the weight even more. Another problem is the efficiency of solar panels. Those that we use today convert only about 20 percent of the sunlight they receive into useable electrical energy.

It is therefore unlikely that we will see solar-powered cars going into commercial production any time soon, and those that do become available will be very expensive. But the news is not all bad. Research into solar-powered cars will almost certainly result in improvements in the efficiency and size of solar cells, which will be useful in many fields where solar energy is applied.

Step 7 Vocabulary View

Choose the definition or synonym for each of the following English words or phrases.

1. vehicle ________
2. horizontal ________
3. capture ________
4. practical ________
5. sufficient ________
6. regularly ________
7. efficiency ________
8. convert ________
9. commercial ________
10. apply ________

a. flat
b. relating to an action in real life
c. car, bus, truck, etc.
d. to catch
e. happening all the time
f. ability to use energy successfully
g. to use
h. enough
i. to change from one thing to another
j. relating to buying and selling

Step 8 Reading Comprehension & Lexicogrammar: Word Choice

Choose (a)-(d) to complete each statement in a grammatically correct sentence so that it matches the content of the passage.

1. Solar-powered cars have large horizontal surfaces ________ they can capture a lot of energy from the sun.
   a. so as b. as a result c. so that d. in order

2. Collecting enough sunlight is one of several practical problems ________ by solar-powered cars.
   a. faced b. faces c. face d. facing

3. Solar panels that are ________ use today are not very efficient at converting sunlight into energy.
   a. on b. in c. at d. by

4. ________ the weight of the car increases, more power is required to operate it.
   a. As b. While c. Though d. After

5. There is ________ doubt that research into solar-powered cars will benefit other fields.
   a. small b. little c. less d. minor

Step 9 Best Summary

Choose the best summary.

1. Advances in technology will soon make it possible to mass-produce solar cars.
2. We will soon see cars resembling those in the World Solar Challenge on normal roads.
3. Solar-powered cars are widely available, but they are too expensive for most people.
4. Several factors make it difficult for solar-powered cars to be commercially successful.
5. The number of solar-powered cars will increase when batteries become lighter.

Step 10 Free Writing & Interviewing

Write your answer for each of the following questions and then ask each other each of the following questions below.

A. What are the characteristics of solar-powered cars compared to regular vehicles?

....

....

....

1. Would you like to drive a solar car? Why?
2. What do you think are the merits and demerits of using solar cars?
3. What other kinds of vehicles or things do you think solar energy should be used for?

B. What are the pros and cons of owning a car?

....

....

....

1. Do you have a driver's license? If not, do you intend to get one?
2. Do you intend to buy a car one day? If so, what kind would you prefer?
3. Do people really need to own a car?

Step 11 Template Essay Writing & Oral Presentation

Follow the template and write on the topic below and read it aloud in pairs or groups.

TOPIC: Do you think gasoline-powered cars will disappear one day?

There are now alternatives to gasoline-powered cars, such as ....

....

....

....

However, it is not so easy to stop producing gasoline-powered cars because .....

....

....

....

All in all, I believe that ....

....

....

....

Step 12 Free Discussion

CD 2-22 ～ 24

Listen to/read the model dialog and talk freely with your partner using the following question.

QUESTION: What are the pros and cons of solar cars?

Model Dialogs

Positive	Negative
A: What are the pros of solar cars? **B:** I think one of the pros is that they don't consume gasoline and don't emit any carbon dioxide. **A:** Exactly. What else? **B:** Unlike gasoline cars, they make no noise. **A:** That's true. But electric cars also produce no noise. **B:** But they use electrical batteries produced mostly by burning fossil fuels.	**A:** What are the cons of solar cars? **B:** I'm not sure, but I guess they are far more expensive than regular gasoline cars. **A:** That's possible, but you don't have to pay for gasoline once you have bought one. **B:** That's true, but maintenance may be troublesome, like cleaning solar panels, and stuff like that. On top of that, they can't run as fast as regular cars. That's not cool.

Useful Patterns for Writing & Speaking from Unit 11

1	What kind of people mostly ～ ?	だいたいどのような人が～をしますか。
2	Where is the goal of ～ ?	～のゴール（到達点、目的地）はどこですか。
3	The challenge of A is just one of several practical problems that B faces.	A の困難は B が直面しているいくつかの実際的問題のひとつに過ぎません。
4	Advances in technology will soon make it possible to ～ .	科学技術が進んで～をすることがすぐ可能になるでしょう。
5	Several factors make it difficult for A to B.	いくつかの要因で A が B をすることは困難です。
6	What are the characteristics of A compared to B?	B と比較して A の特徴は何ですか。
7	What do you think are the merits and demerits of ～ ?	～のメリットとデメリットは何ですか。
8	What are the pros and cons of ～ ?	～の利点と欠点は何ですか。
9	There are now alternatives to A, such as B.	いまでは B など A に代わるものがあります。
10	It is not so easy to stop A because B.	B（節）であるために A を止めることは容易ではないです。

World's First Liquid Hydrogen-Powered Plane Unveiled

水素電池 | 世界初の液体水素エンジン飛行機がお披露目

Have you ever seen cars equipped with hydrogen batteries running on the road? The video shows you an airplane that flies using a liquid-hydrogen engine. How do its characteristics compare with those of conventional jet-powered airplanes? The essay reports on the current state of hydrogen engines in Japan. What obstacles can you think of? Also, point out the good and bad aspects of traveling by air compared to traveling by car, bus or train.

PHASE 1 *WARM UP*

Photo Description

Look at the photo below and choose the sentence that best describes it.

1. Mechanics are working on the engine of a plane.
2. The engine cover has been taken off so we can see inside.
3. Someone is writing something on the side of the plane.
4. The engine is standing on the ground next to the plane.

Vocabulary Preview

Choose the Japanese equivalent for each of the following English words or phrases.

1. liquid hydrogen ______
2. hydrogen-powered ______
3. aviation industry ______
4. net-zero emissions ______
5. breakthrough ______
6. emission-free ______
7. gaseous hydrogen ______
8. fuel cell ______
9. high density ______
10. long-range ______

a. 高密度
b. 水素を動力源にした
c. 突破口、打開策 (=a sudden dramatic development)
d. 航空産業、航空業界
e. ガス状の水素、水素ガス、気体水素
f. 燃料電池
g. 長距離で
h. 二酸化炭素を排出せずに
i. （二酸化炭素）実質無排出
j. 液体水素

PHASE 2 VIEWING & LISTENING

Step 3 Listening for Comprehension: Q&A

Watch the video and answer the following question.  (Time 01:41)

Q: What advantages do liquid hydrogen-powered planes have over regular planes?

A: ....

....

Step 4 Listening for Comprehension: Multiple Choice 

Watch the video again and choose the best answer for each of the following questions.

Q1: Liquid hydrogen can be produced from what?

A. Solar energy **B.** Wind energy
C. Solar and wind energy **D.** Not mentioned

Q2: How much further can a solid hydrogen plane fly than a gaseous one?

A. 1.5 times **B.** More than 2 times **C.** More than three times **D.** Not mentioned

Step 5 Listening for Perception: Word Choice & Fill-in-the-Blanks

Listen to the following part and choose the words you hear or fill in the blanks.   2-27

Narrator: This electric aircraft just completed [1](a/an/the/x) world's first public flight using liquid hydrogen.

Test Pilot Johannes Garbino-Anton: It's super quiet, no vibration. And you can tell it's efficient by just listening to it.

Narrator: Hydrogen flight is one of several competing technologies being explored, as the aviation industry aims for net-zero emissions by [2](________). The world's aviation industry accounted for over [3](________)% of global energy-related CO_2 emissions in [4](________). According to German-based developer H2FLY, this flight may have been the breakthrough needed to prove that hydrogen-powered aviation is the future. Liquid hydrogen can be produced from [5](________) (________) (________) energy, making it emission-free. It also allows the plane to fly for double the amount of time. The plane's maximum range would be roughly [6](________) miles with gaseous hydrogen and around [7](________) with liquid hydrogen. That's enough to fly from Paris to Lisbon. Here's Josef Kallo, founder and CEO of H2FLY.

Josef Kallo: This is a world's first using liquid hydrogen storage with [8](a/an/the/x) fuel cell and an electric motor to propel an aircraft. And this achievement shows us that it is possible not only to fly with hydrogen, which we have shown for hundred times* in the last couple of years, but also to go [9](long-range/longer-range). So, the [10](high/higher) density of the liquid hydrogen gives us the opportunity not only to fly emission-free, but also to fly [11](long-range/longer-range).

* [**hundred times**] 文法的には **hundreds of times** が正しいが、話者の音声を優先

PHASE 3 *LISTENING & READING*

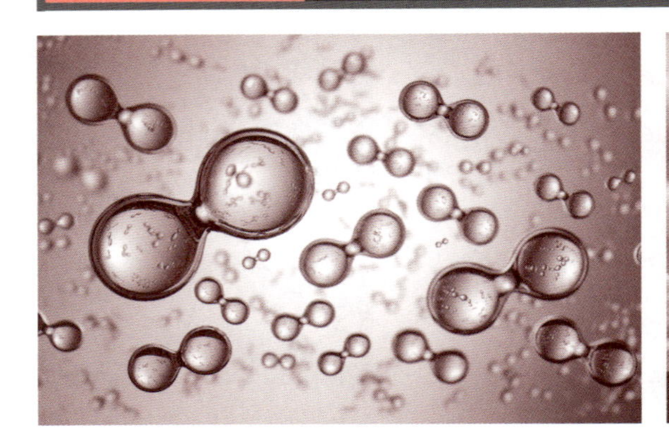

 **Synchro-Reading**  2-28

Listen to the recording and read the following passage silently to understand what is said.

The global passenger aircraft industry is dominated by the US builder Boeing and the European company Airbus. Japan's last commercial aircraft program, the YS-11, was discontinued in 1973. This was Japan's last commercially successful passenger aircraft. In 2007, Mitsubishi Heavy Industries announced a project to develop the Mitsubishi SpaceJet as a passenger aircraft, but this was terminated in 2023. (5)

Nevertheless, Japan is still determined to establish itself as a major player in the global aviation industry. In March 2024, the Japanese Ministry of Economy, Trade, and Industry announced that it plans to invest 4 trillion yen to develop a next-generation hydrogen-powered passenger jet, which is expected to be completed after 2035 in a collaboration between Japan's public and private sectors. (10)

In addition to building a cutting-edge new aircraft, Japan is also hoping that this project will contribute to the decarbonization of air transportation, which has been responsible for a huge amount of carbon emissions. Using hydrogen fuel is a natural choice for this project because when it burns, it emits only water vapor and heat, making it a zero-emissions fuel. The environmental benefit is even greater if the fuel used is so-called "green hydrogen." This is a type of hydrogen produced through the use of renewable energy such as solar and wind power, which means no carbon is emitted in the manufacturing process. (15)

The project faces challenges at present because the costs of producing hydrogen are still high, and the infrastructure for storage and distribution is limited. But if these challenges can be overcome, the prospects for zero-emission aviation look promising. (20)

Vocabulary View

2-29

Choose the definition or synonym for each of the following English words or phrases.

1. dominate ______ a. with a strong will
2. discontinue ______ b. the most advanced; newest; latest; state-of-the-art
3. terminate ______ c. steam
4. determined ______ d. to control
5. collaboration ______ e. able to be made again
6. cutting-edge ______ f. to stop doing
7. vapor ______ g. to deal with and control a problem
8. renewable ______ h. to end
9. overcome ______ i. with good future results
10. promising ______ j. working together

Step 8 Reading Comprehension & Lexicogrammar: Word Choice

Choose (a)-(d) to complete each statement in a grammatically correct sentence so that it matches the content of the passage.

1. The ______ companies in the global aircraft industry are Boeing and Airbus.
   a. dominated b. dominate c. dominant d. dominator

2. The Mitsubishi SpaceJet project ______ to an end in 2023.
   a. came b. arrived c. brought d. led

3. The Japanese government will work ______ with the private sector on the new project.
   a. hand on hand b. hand over hand c. hand with hand d. hand in hand

4. Burning hydrogen emits heat as well as water vapor, which is a harmless ______.
   a. subject b. substance c. matter d. material

5. ______ the costs of producing hydrogen are still high.
   a. Currently b. Momentarily c. Recently d. Lately

Best Summary

Choose the best summary.

1. Japan has become the world leader in hydrogen-fuel technology.
2. Japan is planning to enter the global passenger jet market for the first time.
3. Many aircraft companies want to use "green hydrogen" produced in Japan.
4. Japan is following the trend of developing hydrogen-powered aircraft.
5. Japan plans to build a new hydrogen-powered passenger aircraft.

PHASE 4 *WRITING & SPEAKING*

Step 10 Free Writing & Interviewing

Write your answer for each of the following questions and then ask each other each of the following questions below.

A. Would you like to try a hydrogen flight? Why?

1. What are the pros and cons of traveling by air?
2. What do you think is the biggest problem related to hydrogen-powered flight?
3. Do you think we should be quick to introduce hydrogen-powered flights? Why?

B. Should Japan spend a lot of money on developing an expensive new plane or should it use that money for other priorities?

1. What is the most serious environmental problem in Japan?
2. What is the most serious social problem in Japan?
3. Do you think these problems can be solved with government money?

Template Essay Writing & Oral Presentation

Follow the template and write on the topic below and read it aloud in pairs or groups.

TOPIC: What are the advantages and disadvantages of air travel?

On the one hand, there are a lot of good things about air travel.

Conversely, we can point out some disadvantages.

From my point of view,

Step 12 Free Discussion

CD 2-30 ～ 32

Listen to/read the model dialog and talk freely with your partner using the following question.

QUESTION: Would you like to fly with a hydrogen powered plane?

Model Dialogs

Positive	Negative
A: Would you like to fly in a hydrogen-powered plane? **B:** Definitely. It sounds great. **A:** How so? **B:** It would be great to enjoy a flight with less noise and vibration. I always feel bad when I hear noise coming from the engines and feel constant vibrations on a regular plane. **A:** I feel the same way. But we may have to wait for another 10-20 years to take that kind of flight. **B:** Yes, that's too long to wait.	**A:** Would you like to fly in a hydrogen-powered plane? **B:** No, I'm not interested. **A:** Really? Do you like to fly? **B:** I rarely fly. I don't enjoy flying to other places. In fact, I don't like traveling. **A:** Okay, but do you know anything about hydrogen? Don't you think it would be great if we could make use of hydrogen for our future? **B:** Yes, that sounds wonderful. But I have more important things to think about.

Useful Patterns for Writing & Speaking from Unit 12

1	What advantages does A have over B?	A が B より有利な（優っている）点は何ですか。
2	The A industry is dominated by B.	A 産業(業界) は B に大多数を占められています。
3	A is still determined to establish itself as a major player in the B industry.	A は B 産業（業界）において主要な役割を果たす決意を捨てていません。
4	Using A is a natural choice for B.	A の使用は B にとって当然の選択です。
5	A faces challenges at present because B.	A は B であるため、現在困難に直面しています。
6	What do you think is the biggest problem related to ～ ?	～に関連した最大の問題点は何であると思いますか。
7	Do you think we should be quick to ～ ?	～を急いでするべきであると思いますか。
8	What is the most serious problem in ～ ?	～におけるもっとも深刻な問題は何ですか。
9	Do you know anything about ～ ?	～ついて何かご存じですか。
10	Don't you think it would be great if we could make use of ～ for our future?	～を未来のために利用できれば素晴らしいことであると思いませんか。

UNIT 13 Benin Entrepreneur Harnesses Biowaste to Power Homes, Farms

2-33

バイオ廃棄物 家庭から出る生ごみの有効活用法

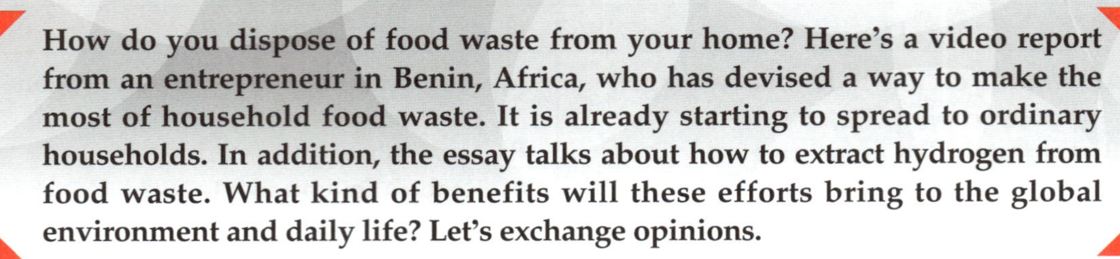

How do you dispose of food waste from your home? Here's a video report from an entrepreneur in Benin, Africa, who has devised a way to make the most of household food waste. It is already starting to spread to ordinary households. In addition, the essay talks about how to extract hydrogen from food waste. What kind of benefits will these efforts bring to the global environment and daily life? Let's exchange opinions.

PHASE 1 *WARM UP*

Step 1 Photo Description

Look at the photo below and choose the sentence that best describes it.

1. The woman is placing pans on the stove.
2. The woman is cooking something in a frying pan.
3. The woman is looking at the two saucepans on the stove.
4. The woman is serving food from the pans.

Step 2 Vocabulary Preview

2-34

Choose the Japanese equivalent for each of the following English words or phrases.

1. entrepreneur	______	a. 家畜
2. harness	______	b. 活用する (=to make use of; utilize)
3. biowaste	______	c. 生分解性廃棄物、バイオ廃棄物
4. food waste	______	d. 泡立て器、(オーブン調理用の) 攪拌機(かくはんき)
5. founder	______	e. 生物ガス、バイオガス
6. livestock	______	f. 創設者 (=originator; creator; initiator)
7. whisk	______	g. 食品廃棄物、フードロス
8. inspire	______	h. 企業家
9. inadvertently	______	i. うっかり (=carelessly; thoughtlessly)
10. biogas	______	j. 刺激を与える (=to stimulate; motivate; encourage)

PHASE 2 *VIEWING & LISTENING*

Listening for Comprehension: Q&A

Watch the video and answer the following question.

(Time 01:29)

Q: What can fuel transformed from food waste be used for?

A: ....

....

Listening for Comprehension: Multiple Choice

Watch the video again and choose the best answer for each of the following questions.

Q1: What is the tank built beneath neighborhoods and industrial zones made of?

A. Concrete **B.** Plastic **C.** Steel **D.** Wood

Q2: What does biogas abundantly contain?

A. Compost **B.** Fertilizer **C.** Fuels **D.** Methane

Step 5

Listening for Perception: Word Choice & Fill-in-the-Blanks

Listen to the following part and choose the words you hear or fill in the blanks.

2-35

Narrator: This food waste is going to be [1](transformed/transforming) into fuel that can once again be used to cook or even heat this home. It's thanks to [2](a/an/the/x) local firm in Benin that's [3](transformed/transforming) everyday biowaste into [4](a/an/the/x) powerful energy source. Enock Gnaga is the founder of Benin Biogas. His team [5](has revolutionized/is revolutionizing) how hundreds of homes and more than [6](a dozen/dozens of) farms manage waste and energy.

Enock Gnaga: On this farm, all the waste from livestock and processing [7](will/would) be recovered as gas products in the logic of being able to power the ovens, the [8](　　　　　　) for the ovens, the cooking, the toasting, but also produce electricity.

Narrator: Benin Biogas has built [9](network/networks) of concrete tanks beneath neighborhoods and industrial zones. They act as reactors, [10](transformed / transforming) organic waste into biogas – a [11](　　　　　　) - (　　　　　　) energy source that now provides fuel for over [12](　　　　　　) households. Gnaga says he was inspired as a student. He watched one day as a candle [13](　　　　　　) fell into his food waste bin.

Enock Gnaga: When it [14](　　　　　　) fire, I thought, what is this? I became interested in this by discussing with my environmental chemistry professor. That's [15](when/where) he told me that it was okay. It's biogas.

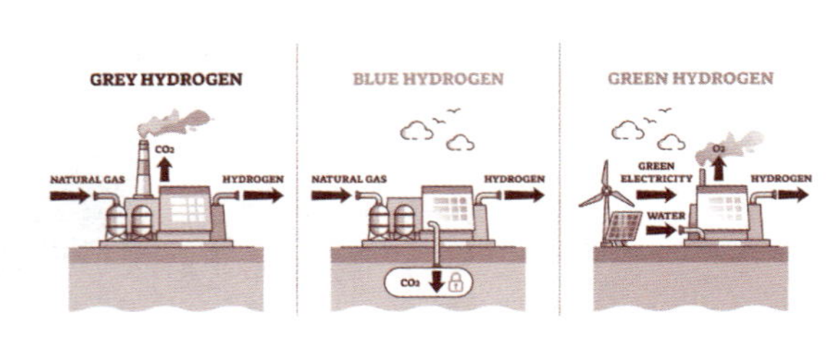

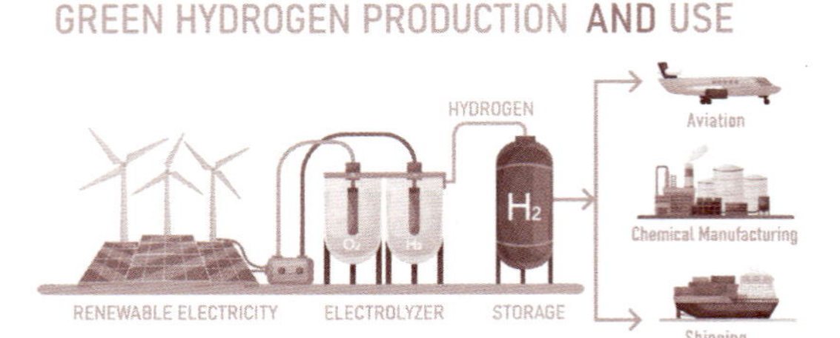

Step 6 Synchro-Reading

2-36

Listen to the recording and read the following passage silently to understand what is said.

Many countries, including Japan, have pledged to achieve net zero in greenhouse gas emissions by 2050. One fuel that could greatly contribute to achieving this target is clean (or "green") hydrogen, which releases no carbon when burned, only water vapor and heat. At present, there is a debate over whether it should be produced using fossil fuels or renewable energy. Now, however, a third option is being discussed: producing clean hydrogen from biowaste. Normally, treating biowaste to produce fuel would result in producing not hydrogen but biogas, which is a combination of methane and carbon dioxide.

Ways2H, a startup company in California, can take trash thrown away by homes and businesses, along with plastics and hazardous medical waste, and convert this material into hydrogen. The company claims that this method enables them to produce hydrogen at a cost of $5 per kilogram. In comparison, the cost of producing one kilogram of hydrogen from wind or solar power is currently between $11 and $16, although this cost is falling.

The main reason the cost is so low is that the company does not have to buy its raw materials. In fact, the opposite is true, because municipalities have to pay a company to take trash away, and so they can use Ways2H to do this.

The CEO of Ways2H says we will eventually need to produce electricity without emitting carbon in the process. In that case, he says, it makes more sense to devote wind and solar resources to electricity generation and to produce hydrogen from waste materials. He believes that waste is capable of producing one third of the world's clean-hydrogen needs.

Step 7 Vocabulary View

2-37

Choose the definition or synonym for each of the following English words or phrases.

1. pledge	______	**a.** to dispose of
2. contribute to	______	**b.** to allocate; to dedicate; to reserve
3. release	______	**c.** to promise
4. vapor	______	**d.** to change; to transform
5. renewable	______	**e.** at the end of a period of time
6. startup company	______	**f.** to play an important part
7. throw away	______	**g.** not lost when used
8. convert	______	**h.** to give out; to emit
9. eventually	______	**i.** a business at the initial stages of its life cycle
10. devote	______	**j.** very small drops of liquid in the air

Step 8 Reading Comprehension & Lexicogrammar: Word Choice

Choose (a)-(d) to complete each statement in a grammatically correct sentence so that it matches the content of the passage.

1. Japan and many other countries have declared a ______ to achieve "net-zero" by 2030.
a. committee **b.** commitment **c.** committal **d.** committing

2. When clean hydrogen is burned, it produces no polluting ______.
a. omissions **b.** missions **c.** remissions **d.** emissions

3. Compared to ______ hydrogen from solar or wind power, the method using biowaste is cheaper.
a. produced **b.** production **c.** producing **d.** produce

4. The main ______ behind the low cost is that the company does not have to purchase raw materials.
a. factor **b.** aspect **c.** situation **d.** issue

5. The CEO believes that waste has the ______ to produce one third of the world's hydrogen needs.
a. possibility **b.** probability **c.** potential **d.** prospect

Best Summary

Choose the best summary.

1. Ways2H can convert biogas into hydrogen.
2. Ways2H can convert trash into hydrogen at low cost.
3. California has the cheapest raw materials for making hydrogen.
4. Ways2H is producing hydrogen using solar and wind power.
5. California is now the world center for hydrogen production.

Step 10 Free Writing & Interviewing

Write your answer for each of the following questions and then ask each other each of the following questions below.

A. How would you evaluate the food waste technology?

1. What interests you most about this technology?
2. Do you think this technology should be used in Japan?
3. In what other areas do you think this technology can be applied?

B. Do you think Japan should make more effort to use alternative sources of energy such as wind or solar power?

1. Would you like to live in a house with solar panels for producing electricity?
2. How would you feel to see many large wind turbines starting to appear in open spaces around Japan?
3. In what ways could we cut our power consumption in daily life?

Step 11 Template Essay Writing & Oral Presentation

Follow the template and write on the topic below and read it aloud in pairs or groups.

TOPIC: Should we make efforts toward using alternative sources of energy?

There are several sources of alternative energy such as

It will not be easy to use these on a wide scale because of various reasons.

Speaking for myself, I would like to

Step 12 Free Discussion

2-38 ～ 40

Listen to/read the model dialog and talk freely with your partner using the following question.

QUESTION: Do you think this technology will spread throughout the world?

Model Dialogs

Positive	Negative
A: Do you think this technology will spread throughout the world? **B:** Yes, I think so. **A:** What makes you think that? **B:** I think the technology is attractive enough for companies to produce devices to utilize biowaste and their products are likely to attract people. **A:** So, you think the device will sell well. **B:** I'm sure people will realize that we can use biowaste to reduce carbon emissions.	**A:** Do you think this technology will spread throughout the world? **B:** No, I don't think so. **A:** How come? **B:** I don't think people want to be bothered by dealing with biowaste. **A:** What do you mean? **B:** Nowadays, people are too busy to pay attention to what they use and throw away. They have more important things to consider if they want to get ahead in life.

Useful Patterns for Writing & Speaking from Unit 13

1	What does ～ abundantly contain?	～には何がたくさん含まれていますか。
2	I became interested in A by B-ing.	私はBをしてAに興味を持つようになりました。
3	At present, there is a debate over whether A should B.	現在AはBをすべきであるかどうか議論されています。
4	A is now the world center for B production.	AはいまやBの生産の世界的中心地です。
5	What interests you most about ～ ?	～について何にもっとも興味がありますか。
6	Do you think A should make more effort to B?	AはもっとBをする努力をするべきであると思いますか。
7	How would you feel to see A starting to B?	AはBをし始めるのを見たらどう思いますか。
8	Do you think ～ will spread throughout the world?	～が世界各国に広がっていくと思いますか。
9	I think A is attractive enough for B to C.	AはBがCをするほど魅力があると思いますか。
10	Nowadays, people are too busy to pay attention to ～ .	最近、人は忙し過ぎて～に注意を払えません。

Trafficked Wildlife Find Safe Haven at US Zoos

動物保護 密輸された野生動物が米国の動物園で保護される

Do you have any pets? In Japan, dogs, cats, turtles, and goldfish are popular pets, but overseas, the range of pets is wider and there is even a high demand for rare or endangered animals. The video explains how animals are illegally smuggled. The essay delves further into the current situation. What role do you expect social media to play to stop illegal animal trading? Also, what benefits do you think you can get from keeping pets?

PHASE 1 *WARM UP*

Photo Description

Look at the photo below and choose the sentence that best describes it.

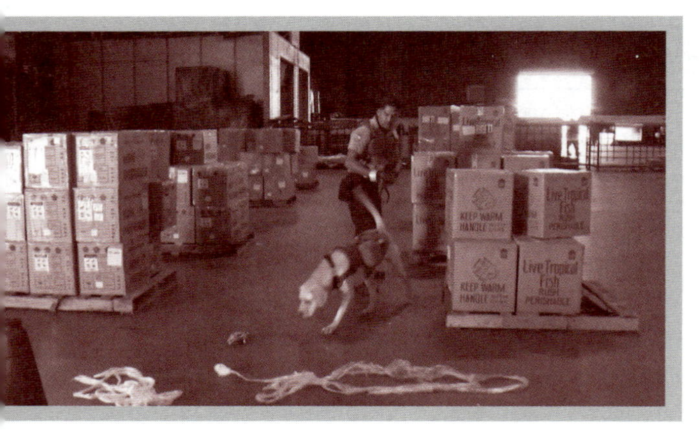

1. A man and a dog are working inside a warehouse.
2. The dog is climbing up on some boxes.
3. The man is opening boxes for the dog to check.
4. The man is trying to catch the dog.

Vocabulary Preview

Choose the Japanese equivalent for each of the following English words or phrases.

1. trafficking ______
2. thrive ______
3. confiscations ______
4. greed ______
5. epicenter ______
6. criminal referrals ______
7. essence ______
8. (customs) clearance ______
9. urgent ______
10. potential ______

a. 欲、貪欲、欲望 (=intense and selfish desire)
b. 繁栄する、繁殖する (=to prosper; flourish)
c. 犯罪照会、刑事照会(警察の捜査のための情報収集)
d. 潜在的な (=possible; probable; likely)
e. 通関(手続き)
f. 緊急の (=emergency)
g. 押収、没収
h. 重要性、本質、特質 (=nature)
i. 中心点、震源地 (=center)
j. 密輸、密売 (=illegal trading)

PHASE 2 *VIEWING & LISTENING*

Step 3 Listening for Comprehension: Q&A

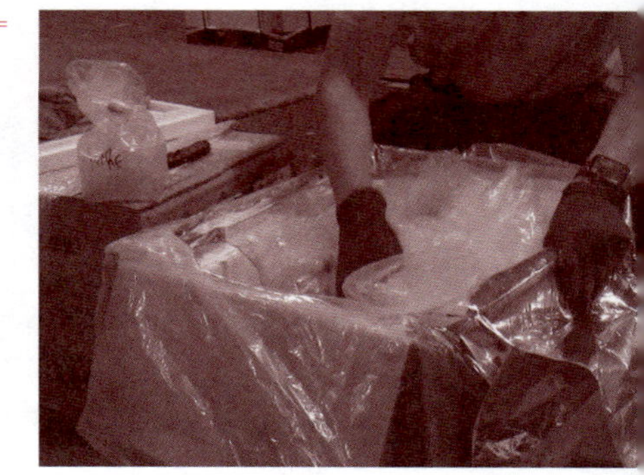

Watch the video and answer the following question.

(Time 01:33)

Q: How are wild animals protected?

A: ....

....

Listening for Comprehension: Multiple Choice

WEB動画 DVD

Watch the video again and choose the best answer for each of the following questions.

Q1: What is essential to save the lives of live animals when they are refused entry at ports?
A. Efficiency **B.** Greed **C.** Potential **D.** Speed

Q2: Where will most confiscated animals be kept?
A. At airports **B.** At aquariums or zoos **C.** At care facilities **D.** In luggage areas

Listening for Perception: Word Choice & Fill-in-the-Blanks

Listen to the following part and choose the words you hear or fill in the blanks. WEB動画 DVD  2-43

Narrator: These animals at the Los Angeles Zoo were rescued from the illegal wildlife trafficking trade. As [1](a/an/the/x) part of a major effort to make sure animals [2](called/caught) up in the trade can survive and thrive, the U.S. Fish and Wildlife Service has partnered with the Association of Zoos and Aquariums to launch a pilot project. It's called the Wildlife Confiscations Network. Dan Ashe is the president and [3](a/an/the/x) CEO of the Association of Zoos and Aquariums.

Dan Ashe: Wildlife trafficking is [4](________) in greed. It's [5](________) in human need and greed. And these animals are being trafficked all around the world, basically for [6](profit/profits). And we're seeing criminal syndicates who are [7](developed/ developing) around the trafficking of animals. And so it's going to take, it takes a huge [8](collaboration/cooperation) to deal with it.

Narrator: The pilot launched last week in Southern California, which is considered an epicenter for [9](trafficked/trafficking) wildlife. The goal of the program is to create a group of trusted care facilities that can provide immediate care and housing for animals [10](trafficked/trafficking) through the U.S., according to the Association of Zoos and Aquariums. Between [11](________) (________) (________), the Fish and Wildlife Service had to find care and homes for nearly [12](________) trafficked animals linked to more than [13](________) criminal referrals. [14](________) is of the essence when live animals are refused clearance at [15](a/an/the/x) ports. They require urgent care from experts to survive and to stop the [16](spread/spreading) of potential diseases.

PHASE 3 *LISTENING & READING*

Synchro-Reading

2-44

Listen to the recording and read the following passage silently to understand what is said.

The illegal wildlife trade, or wildlife trafficking as it is also known, is a worldwide problem. It can involve killing animals, often rare or endangered species, for their skins or body parts. Ivory from elephant tusks or the horns from rhinos are particularly popular. Animals are also trapped so that they can be sold to people who want to own 5 exotic pets. For example, there is a great demand for big cats such as cheetahs as well as certain species of ape, which can cost as much as $20,000 per animal. They are often smuggled across multiple national borders in secret compartments in luggage, shipping containers, or vehicles.

In recent years, the huge growth of social media has helped illegal wildlife traders to 10 easily reach potential buyers. Meta, the parent company of Facebook, has a strict policy that bans listings promoting the buying or selling of animals or animal products, and the company will remove any posts that it finds violating this rule. Several tech companies, including Meta, have been working with the World Wildlife Fund (WWF) to try to eliminate the problem. Together, they try to identify new keyword search terms used by 15 illegal wildlife traders so that listings can be taken down.

However, the criminal groups who are responsible for illegal trading have no trouble thinking of ingenious new ways to avoid detection. It is therefore difficult – perhaps even impossible – for social media companies to keep up with the enormous number of such listings, which means that buying and selling animals through social media platforms is 20 an ongoing problem.

Vocabulary View

2-45

Choose the definition or synonym for each of the following English words or phrases.

1. trafficking	______	a. an enclosed space
2. tusk	______	b. to take secretly into a country
3. smuggle	______	c. long curved tooth
4. compartment	______	d. a person who buys and sells goods
5. eliminate	______	e. extremely clever
6. trader	______	f. very large; huge
7. ingenious	______	g. finding; discovery
8. detection	______	h. illegal buying and selling
9. enormous	______	i. to take away; to get rid of
10. ongoing	______	j. happening now

Step 8 Reading Comprehension & Lexicogrammar: Word Choice

Choose (a)-(d) to complete each statement in a grammatically correct sentence so that it matches the content of the passage.

1. Rare or endangered species of animals are ______ risk because of the illegal wildlife trade.
   a. at b. on c. with d. in

2. Animals such as big cats or apes are trapped to ______ to the demand for exotic pets.
   a. order b. supply c. respond d. settle

3. Criminals often ______ animals in secret compartments to smuggle them across national borders.
   a. concern b. conceal c. confirm d. contact

4. The criminal groups ______ illegal trading are skilled at avoiding detection.
   a. around b. over c. beside d. behind

5. The number of listings for illegal trades is ______ great that social media companies cannot keep up.
   a. such b. so c. as d. very

Best Summary

Choose the best summary.

1. Illegal wildlife traders are looking for ways other than social media to advertise.
2. The WWF is making great progress in preventing wildlife trafficking.
3. The WWF uses social media postings to inform people about wildlife trafficking.
4. It is hard for social media companies to stop wildlife traffickers from using their sites.
5. Buying and selling animals online used to be a more serious problem than it is now.

PHASE 4 *WRITING & SPEAKING*

Step 10 Free Writing & Discussion

Write your answer for each of the following questions and then ask each other each of the following questions below.

A. What are the pros and cons of keeping a pet?

....

....

....

1. Have you ever kept a pet? Why do you think people keep pets?
2. Are you attracted to a rare species? Would you like to have one of them at home?
3. What is the best way to stop wildlife trafficking?

B. What do you think are some of the negative aspects of social media?

....

....

....

1. Could you go for one day without checking social media?
2. Have you ever had any problems using social media?
3. What is an appropriate length of time to use social media each day?

Step 11 Template Essay Writing & Oral Presentation

Follow the template and write on the topic below and read it aloud in pairs or groups.

TOPIC: The pros and cons of keeping a pet

There are many reasons people choose to keep a pet including ....

....

....

....

The reason I (don't) keep a pet is very simple. ....

....

....

....

On the whole, I think that keeping pets is ....

....

....

....

Step 12 Free Discussion

CD 2-46 ～ 48

Listen to/read the model dialog and talk freely with your partner using the following question.

QUESTION: How can we stop the wildlife trafficking trade?

Model Dialogs

Positive	Negative
A: How can we stop the wildlife trafficking trade? **B:** Well, where there is demand, there will always be supply. We need to tackle that demand. **A:** Absolutely, but how? **B:** Governments should try to raise awareness about suffering animals. **A:** Is that enough? **B:** Illegal trading of wildlife should be strictly banned with severe punishments.	**A:** How can we stop the wildlife trafficking trade? **B:** I would say it is impossible to terminate illegal trading. **A:** Why do you think so? **B:** As long as it is profitable, someone will continue to do it. **A:** Don't you think we should punish violators more severely? **B:** It might be effective to some extent, but it won't work completely.

Useful Patterns for Writing & Speaking from Unit 14

1	What is essential to ～ ?	～するのに不可欠なことは何ですか。
2	What are the pros and cons of ～ ?	～をすることの利点と欠点(長所と短所)は何ですか。
3	What is the best way to stop ～ ?	～をやめさせる最善策は何ですか。
4	How can we stop ～ ?	～はどうすればやめさせることができますか。
5	Have you ever had any problems –ing?	～をする上で何か問題が起きたことがありますか。
6	There are many reasons people ～ .	人が～をするのは様々な理由があるからです。
7	Governments should try to raise awareness about ～ .	～に関する意識を政府は高めようとすべきです。
8	～ should be strictly banned with severe punishments.	～はもっと厳しく罰せられるべきです。
9	I would say it is impossible to ～ .	～をするのは不可能でしょうね。
10	Don't you think we should punish ～ more severely?	～をもっと厳しく罰すべきであると思いませんか。

Lake Geneva's Plastic Pollution as High as World's Oceans

 2-49

プラゴミ スイスの湖でプラスチックゴミが大量発生

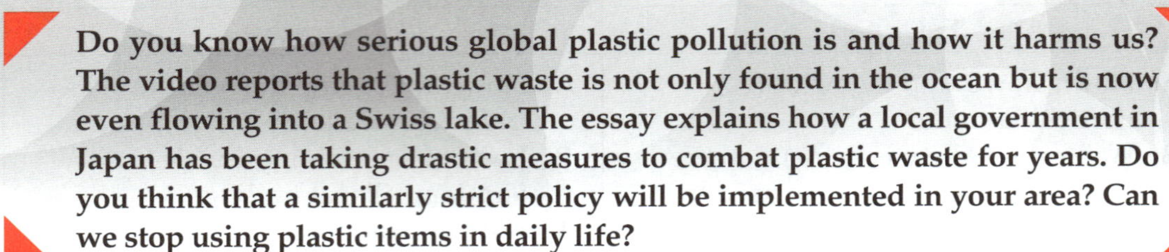

Do you know how serious global plastic pollution is and how it harms us? The video reports that plastic waste is not only found in the ocean but is now even flowing into a Swiss lake. The essay explains how a local government in Japan has been taking drastic measures to combat plastic waste for years. Do you think that a similarly strict policy will be implemented in your area? Can we stop using plastic items in daily life?

PHASE 1 *WARM UP*

Photo Description

Look at the photo below and choose the sentence that best describes it.

1. Several boats are sailing around the harbor.
2. The boat has a tall mast but no sails.
3. The surface of the water is rough with high waves.
4. The boat is tied up securely on the shore.

Vocabulary Preview

 2-50

Choose the Japanese equivalent for each of the following English words or phrases.

1. reputation	______	**a.** 船尾
2. non-profit	______	**b.** 残留物 (=leftovers; remains)
3. stern	______	**c.** 悲観的な (=negative) ↔楽観的な (=optimistic)
4. particles	______	**d.** 無作法、無礼
5. fragments	______	**e.** 粒子
6. residue	______	**f.** 認知、認識 (=recognition)
7. incivility	______	**g.** 評判 (=a generally held widespread opinion)
8. ditch	______	**h.** 捨てる、廃棄する (=to throw out [away]; dispose of)
9. pessimistic	______	**i.** 断片、かけら (=tiny pieces)
10. awareness	______	**j.** 非営利（団体）

PHASE 2 VIEWING & LISTENING

Listening for Comprehension: Q&A

Watch the video and answer the following question.

(Time 01:40)

Q: Why has plastic pollution got worse in Lake Geneva?

A: ....

....

Listening for Comprehension: Multiple Choice

Watch the video again and choose the best answer for each of the following questions.

Q1: What is the major pollutant?

A. Bottles B. Food packaging C. Furniture D. Tire residue

Q2: What or who does the man say is most responsible for plastic pollution?

A. Climate change B. Stores and restaurants C. Factories D. Individuals

Step 5 Listening for Perception: Word Choice & Fill-in-the-Blanks

Listen to the following part and choose the words you hear or fill in the blanks.

2-51

Narrator: Switzerland's Lake Geneva has [1](a/an/the/x) reputation for its clean water. It sits at the foot of the Alps and looks postcard ready. But it [2](turns/turned) out plastic pollution here is just as severe as the world's oceans. So how did one of [3](a/an/the/x) Europe's largest lakes become so polluted? Oceaneye, a Geneva-based non-profit, has been collecting plastics from [4](a/an/the/x) oceans for more than a decade. But in 2018 they turned their attention [5](close/closer) to home and conducted their first study in Lake Geneva. That's Pascal Hagmann, Oceaneye's founder. On the stern of a sailing boat, he's using a device to help collect different types of [6](plastic/plastics). There are microplastics – which are small particles of bigger objects – and mesoplastics, which are bigger fragments. Hagmann says [7](____________) (____________) is the major pollutant, followed by food [8](packages/packaging). And that the plastics that end up here aren't just a Switzerland problem, it's a global one. As Lake Geneva [9](border/borders) France and its water eventually flows into the Mediterranean Sea.

Hagmann: [10](A/An/The/x) whole part of that waste comes from people's incivility. People who don't put their waste in a trash can, who [11](____________) them in nature or leave trash overflowing. And that plastic waste is what we're finding in Lake Geneva.

Narrator: Hagmann says projections are pessimistic. And that if the world continues to produce [12](plastic/plastics) at the current rate, we'll produce more than [13](____________) (____________) tons of it per year. But on the [14](bright/brighter) side, he says awareness of the issue is [15](glowing/growing).

PHASE 3 *LISTENING & READING*

Synchro-Reading

Listen to the recording and read the following passage silently to understand what is said.

Plastic waste has become one of the most pressing global environmental problems. National governments and international bodies have been trying to come up with solutions to deal with it. But small local communities have also made effective contributions.

One such community is Kameoka, a city in Kyoto prefecture with a population of around 88,000 people. In 2020, it became the first city in Japan to ban the use of plastic bags at checkout registers in retail stores such as supermarkets and convenience stores.

The city was prompted to take action against plastic bags because of the problem of plastic pollution in the local Hozu River, which runs through the city. Boat trips from here to Arashiyama in Kyoto have long been a popular tourist attraction, but the large amount of plastic waste floating near the riverbanks was spoiling the scenery as well as potentially affecting the river's ecosystem. So, in 2018, the city authorities introduced what they called the "Kameoka Zero Plastic Waste Declaration," in which they committed to discontinuing the use of disposable plastics by 2030.

In 2019, the city started charging for plastic bags, and then in 2020, it banned them altogether. There was some initial resistance to the new ordinance on the part of local residents and business owners, and the city received complaints that the new system made shopping inconvenient. But by February 2021, most of the city's 700 retail stores were cooperating, and an estimated 98 percent of shoppers had started bringing their own bags when they went shopping.

Step 7 Vocabulary View

2-53

Choose the definition or synonym for each of the following English words or phrases.

1. pressing	______	**a.** hills, mountains, rivers, etc.
2. come up with	______	**b.** an expression of dissatisfaction
3. population	______	**c.** to ask money for something
4. prompt	______	**d.** to think of (an idea or plan)
5. spoil	______	**e.** to work together
6. scenery	______	**f.** the number of people living somewhere
7. charge	______	**g.** urgent
8. initial	______	**h.** to make bad
9. complaint	______	**i.** at the beginning
10. cooperate	______	**j.** to make someone act

Step 8 Reading Comprehension & Lexicogrammar: Word Choice

Choose (a)-(d) to complete each statement in a grammatically correct sentence so that it matches the content of the passage.

1. Governments and international bodies have been trying to ______ solutions to the problem of waste.
a. defy **b.** devise **c.** define **d.** defend

2. Retail stores in Kameoka are ______ allowed to supply plastic bags at cash registers.
a. no more **b.** no further **c.** no longer **d.** no way

3. Some years ago, plastic waste ______ the local Hozu River.
a. was polluted **b.** was polluting **c.** pollutes **d.** is polluted

4. The plastic waste was having a negative ______ on the river's ecosystem.
a. effect **b.** affect **c.** infect **d.** defect

5. At first, some residents and business owners were unhappy ______ the new rules.
a. for **b.** to **c.** by **d.** with

Step 9 Best Summary

Choose the best summary.

1. After some early problems, Kameoka's anti-waste measures have proved successful.

2. Kameoka's example has been copied by many towns and cities in Japan.

3. Communities along the Hozu River cooperated to deal with the problem of waste.

4. The number of visitors to Kameoka has increased since the anti-waste measures went into effect.

5. Every business in Kameoka is now an enthusiastic supporter of the anti-waste measures.

PHASE 4 *WRITING & SPEAKING*

Step 10 Free Writing & Interviewing

Write your answer for each of the following questions and then ask each other each of the following questions below.

A. What is the best way to solve the problem of plastic pollution?

....

....

....

1. What do you know about plastic garbage pollution?
2. Why do you think many items are made of plastics?
3. What are the merits and demerits of using plastics for products?

B. Are you careful about sorting your trash and disposing of it correctly?

....

....

....

1. Do you think your city is good at coping with trash in an environmentally friendly way?
2. Do you always put your trash out at the correct time?
3. How can you try to reduce the amount of waste you produce?

Step 11 Template Essay Writing & Oral Presentation

Follow the template and write on the topic below and read it aloud in pairs or groups.

TOPIC: We should try to stop using plastic items in daily life.

Plastic waste causes all kinds of environmental problems. ....

....

....

....

However, plastic is an important part of our daily lives. ....

....

....

....

In conclusion, I would say that ....

....

....

....

Step 12 Free Discussion

CD 2-54 ～ 56

Listen to/read the model dialog and talk freely with your partner using the following question.

QUESTION: Are you doing something to solve the problem of plastic pollution?

Model Dialogs

Positive	Negative
A: Are you doing something to solve the problem of plastic pollution? **B:** Yes, I am. **A:** What are you doing? **B:** I try not to buy plastic products. **A:** How can you do that? **B:** Well, looking at items sold at supermarkets or convenience stores, many items are over-wrapped. But if you look around carefully, you can see a lot of items that are sold unwrapped or unpacked, such as vegetables and fruits. I'm trying to buy unwrapped items as much as possible.	**A:** Are you doing something to solve the problem of plastic pollution? **B:** Not really. I don't know where to begin. **A:** Well, as a consumer, you might want to avoid packaged products at stores or supermarkets. **B:** I can try. I usually separate combustible and incombustible waste at home. **A:** That's a good start. **B:** But what we can do is rather limited. It's all up to companies that produce plastic products. They should reduce or even stop producing plastic items and use other environmentally friendly materials for packaging.

Useful Patterns for Writing & Speaking from Unit 15

1	A has a reputation for its B.	A は B に関して高い評価を受けています。
2	A is not just a B's problem; it's a global one.	A は B の問題に留まらず、地球全体の問題です。
3	～ has become one of the most pressing global environmental problems.	～は最も差し迫った地球全体の環境問題のひとつになっています。
4	The number of A has increased since B.	A の数は B 以来増えています。
5	What is the best way to solve the problem of ～ ?	～の問題解決の最善策は何ですか。
6	What do you know about ～ ?	～についてあなたは何をご存じですか。
7	What are the merits and demerits of ～ ?	～のメリットとデメリットは何ですか。
8	Are you careful about ～ ?	～についてあなたは気を付けていますか。
9	Do you think A is good at B?	A は B をするのが得意であると思いますか。
10	Are you doing something to solve the problem of ～ ?	～の問題解決のためにあなたは何かしていますか。

付録１　ディスカッションに役立つ英語表現

1 主張・説明

1-1 個人的意見を述べる　CD 2-57

1	I would say that ____.	〜であると思います。
2	In my opinion, ____. I'm of the opinion that ____.	私の意見では、〜であります。
3	In my view, ____. From my point of view, ____.	私の見解では、〜であります。
4	As far as I'm concerned, ____.	私に関して言えば、〜であります。
5	Personally, ____.	個人的には、〜であります。

1-2 強い信念を述べる　CD 2-58

1	I really think that ____.	〜であると強く思います。
2	I believe that ____. It is my belief that ____.	〜であると信じています。
3	I firmly believe that ____. I strongly believe that ____.	〜であると強く信じています。
4	I'm sure that ____. I'm certain that ____.	〜であると確信しています。
5	I have no doubt that ____. No doubt ____.	〜であることに疑いの余地がありません。

1-3 推量・憶測を述べる　CD 2-59

1	I guess that ____.	〜であると憶測します。
2	Maybe ____. Perhaps ____.	たぶん〜であるかも知れません。
3	It is possible that ____. It could be that ____.	〜である可能性はあります。
4	I'm not sure, but probably ____. I can't be certain, but ____. It's hard to say for sure, but ____.	確信はないですが、たぶん〜であると思います。
5	I may be wrong, but I think that ____.	間違っているかも知れませんが、〜であると思います。

1-4 提案（助言、説得）する CD 2-60

1	You might want to ____. It could be a good idea to ____. It might be a good idea to ____. One thing you could consider is____. One thing you could do is____. One possibility would be that ____. Would you consider –ing?	～をしてみてはいかがでしょうか。
2	How about –ing? What about –ing?	～をしてはいかがですか。
3	Have you ever thought about –ing?	～をしようと思ったことはありますか。
4	Why don't you ____?	～をしてはいかがですか。
5	You should ____. You ought to ____.	～をすべきです。

2 質問

2-1 特定する CD 2-61

1	What is the point? What is your point?	要はどういうことですか。
2	What is your conclusion?	あなたの結論は何ですか。
3	What are the pros and cons of ____? What are the merits and demerits of ____? What are the advantages and disadvantages of ____? What are the good points and bad points of ____?	～の利点（長所）と欠点（短所）は何ですか。
4	What are the strengths and weaknesses of ____?	～の強みと弱みは何ですか。

2-2 賛否を確認する CD 2-62

1	Are you for or against ____? Do you agree or disagree with ____? Do you support or object to ____?	～に賛成ですか、反対ですか。
2	Regarding ____, which side of the argument are you on? Regarding ____, which side of the argument do you support?	～に関してどちらの議論に賛同しますか。

2-3 意見を聞く CD 2-63

1	What do you think about [of] _____? What's your take on _____? How do you find _____? How do you like _____? How do you feel about _____?	～をどう思いますか。
2	What is your opinion on _____?	～に関してどんな意見をお持ちですか。
3	Can you give me your view(s) on _____?	～に関する意見を聞かせていただけますか。
4	How do you evaluate _____? What is your evaluation on _____? What is your assessment on _____?	～をどう評価しますか。

2-4 意味を確認する CD 2-64

1	What do you mean?	どういう意味ですか。
2	What do you mean by _____?	～とはどういう意味ですか。
3	Do you mean _____? You mean _____? Are you saying that _____? So, what you're saying is that _____? Am I correct in thinking that _____?	～であるということですか。
4	So, to paraphrase your argument, _____?	言い換えると、～であるということですか。
5	Are you insinuating that _____?*	(不愉快なこと) ～であるとでも言いたいのですか。 *喧嘩腰の言い方なので使い方に注意

2-5 要求する、懇願する CD 2-65

1	Could you do me a favor?	お願いことがあるのですか。
2	Would it be possible for you to _____? I was wondering if you could _____. I wonder if you'd mind –ing?	～をしていただくことは可能ですか。
3	May I ask you to _____?	～をしていただけるようお願いできますか。
4	Could you possibly _____?	～をしていただくわけにはいきませんか。
5	I would appreciate it if you could _____.	～をしていただければ幸いです。

3 返答・反応

3-1 同意する 2-66

1	I think so. I agree. You are right. That's right. That's correct.	そう思います。
2	I think so too.	私もそう思います。
3	Maybe you are right. That's possible.	そうかも知れません。
4	Absolutely. Definitely. I couldn't agree more. I completely concur. You are absolutely right. You can say that again. That's spot on.	まったく同感です。
5	You've raised an interesting point.	興味深いポイント（指摘）ですね。

3-2 反対する 2-67

1	I'm sorry, but _____. I'm afraid, _____.	お言葉ですが、～。
2	I don't entirely agree. I'm not sure that's strictly accurate. I think you'll find that's not entirely correct.	完全には同意（賛同）できません。
3	I don't think so. I disagree.	そうは思いません。
4	My take on this is a bit different. Actually, I see things a little differently. I tend to see the matter somewhat differently.	この件について私の考えはちょっと違います。
5	On the contrary, I think that _____.	反対に、私は～であると思います。
6	Absolutely not. Definitely not.	全く違います。
7	That's impossible.	それは不可能です。 それはあり得ません。
8	You could look at it that way, but _____.	そういう見方も可能かも知れませんが、～。

3-3 曖昧に答える・コメントしない CD 2-68

1	I'm not sure.	どうでしょう。 よくわかりません。
2	I don't know.	わかりません。
3	That's not something I could answer.	それは私には答えられません。
4	I have no comment. No comment.	ノーコメントです。
5	Who knows? No one knows.	誰にもわかりません。 / 誰も知りません。
6	Who knows?	誰にわかると言うのですか。 誰が知っていると言うのですか。
7	That's not something that concerns me.	私には興味がないことです。
8	I have no opinion one way or the other.	私にはまったく意見がないです。
9	Give me some time to think about that.	考える時間を少々ください。

付録 2　英語感想文（小論文）の書き方

英語ニュースを聞いたり、ビデオを見た後にコメントする時に役立つ表現をまとめました。

1: OPENING STATEMENT

[ ] I would like to write my comments on the video I watched today.
[ ] I would like to express my idea about the video I watched today.

2: COMMENTING EXPRESSIONS

[ ] 感動 I was impressed by the TV program [the video/the documentary].
[ ] 驚嘆 I was surprised [astonished] by the TV program [the video/the documentary].
[ ] 歓喜 I was pleased with the TV program [the video/the documentary].
[ ] 悲観 I was saddened [depressed] by the TV program [the video/the documentary].

3: EXPRESSING IDEAS

[ ] 思想 I think [believe] that
[ ] 仮定 I assume [guess] that
[ ] 気分 I feel that/I feel like –ing
[ ] 賛成 I am for/I agree with [to] /I support
[ ] 反対 I am against/I disagree with/I object to/I oppose
[ ] 疑問 Why ____?/Why is it that ____?/How come ____?
[ ] 疑問 I don't know why/I don't understand why

4: THESIS STATEMENT

[ ] I would like to show you the reasons.
[ ] I have three reasons why I am against the plan.
[ ] I support the project for the following three reasons.
[ ] Let me write some reasons why I disagree.
[ ] There are three reasons why I think so.

5: LINKING WORDS & PHRASES

[ ] 開始　First/At first/In the first place/To begin with /In the end/Finally/Lastly
[ ] 比較　In comparison/In contrast/Similarly/in comparison to/compared to [with]
[ ] 反駁　But/However/Yet/Nevertheless/On the other hand/On the contrary
[ ] 追加　Moreover/Furthermore/In addition
[ ] 因果　For this reason/That's why ____.
[ ] 結果　As a result/Consequently/Therefore/Thus/Accordingly
[ ] 例証　For example/For instance
[ ] 言換　In other words/That is to say
[ ] 当然　Naturally/Of course/Certainly/Fortunately/Unfortunately/Undoubtedly
[ ] 私見　In my opinion/As far as I'm concerned/I would say ____.
[ ] 結論　In conclusion

6: CONCLUDING WORDS & PHRASES

[ ] In conclusion/In short/To sum up

付録3　国連加盟国一覧表

A
Afghanistan
Albania
Algeria
Andorra
Angola
Antigua and Barbuda
Argentina
Armenia
Australia
Austria
Azerbaijan
B
The Bahamas
Bahrain
Bangladesh
Barbados
Belarus
Belgium
Belize
Benin
Bhutan
Bolivia
Bosnia and Herzegovina
Botswana
Brazil
Brunei
Bulgaria
Burkina Faso
Burundi
C
Cambodia
Cameroon
Canada
Cape Verde
Central African Republic
Chad
Chile
China
Colombia
Comoros
Democratic Republic of the Congo
Republic of the Congo
Costa Rica
Croatia
Cuba
Cyprus
Czech Republic
D
Denmark
Djibouti
Dominica
Dominican Republic
E
East Timor
Ecuador
Egypt
Equatorial Guinea
Eritrea
Estonia
Eswatini
Ethiopia
F
Fiji
Finland
France
G
Gabon
The Gambia
Georgia
Germany
Ghana
Grenada
Guatemala
Guinea
Guinea-Bissau
Guyana
H
Haiti
Honduras
Hungary
I
Iceland
India
Indonesia
Iran
Iraq
Republic of Ireland
Israel
Italy
Ivory Coast
J
Jamaica
Japan
Jordan
K
Kazakhstan
Kenya
Kiribati
Kuwait
Kyrgyzstan
L
Laos
Latvia
Lebanon
Lesotho
Liberia
Libya
Liechtenstein
Lithuania
Luxembourg
M
Madagascar
Malawi
Malaysia
Maldives
Mali
Malta
Marshall Islands
Mauritania
Mauritius
Mexico
Federated States of Micronesia
Moldova
Monaco
Mongolia
Montenegro
Morocco
Mozambique
Myanmar
N
Namibia
Nauru
Nepal
Kingdom of the Netherlands
New Zealand
Nicaragua
Niger
Nigeria
North Korea
North Macedonia
Norway
O
Oman
P
Pakistan
Palau
Panama
Papua New Guinea
Paraguay
Peru
Philippines
Poland
Portugal
Q
Qatar
R
Romania
Russia
Rwanda
S
Saint Kitts and Nevis
Saint Lucia
Saint Vincent and the Grenadines
El Salvador
Samoa
San Marino
São Tomé and Príncipe
Saudi Arabia
Senegal
Serbia
Seychelles
Sierra Leone
Singapore
Slovakia
Slovenia
Solomon Islands
Somalia
South Africa
South Korea
South Sudan
Spain
Sri Lanka
Sudan
Suriname
Sweden
Switzerland
Syria
T
Tajikistan
Tanzania
Thailand
Togo
Tonga
Trinidad and Tobago
Tunisia
Turkey
Turkmenistan
Tuvalu
U
Uganda
Ukraine
United Arab Emirates
United Kingdom
United States
Uruguay
Uzbekistan
V
Vanuatu
Venezuela
Vietnam
Y
Yemen
Z
Zambia
Zimbabwe

付録4　注意すべきアメリカ英語とイギリス英語の相違点

	アメリカ英語 （アメリカ、カナダ）	イギリス英語 （英国、豪州、ニュージーランド、南ア、香港、シンガポール）
発音	bottom /ɑ/ college /ɑ/ dot /ɑ/ fire / r / paper / r / park / r / often /x/	bottom /ɔ/ college /ɔ/ dot /ɔ/ fire /x/ paper /x/ park /x/ often /t/
綴り	center color program organize defense	centre colour programme organise defence
ドットの有無	U.N. U.S.A. U.K.	UN USA UK
語彙	apartment advertisement / ad bathroom / restroom / washroom（カナダ） blinker cookie commencement editorial elevator crosswalk ESL は外国語としての英語（教育）を総じて指す fall freshman sophomore junior senior gas station go on vacation hood parking lot president sick the first floor track truck	flat advert toilet winker biscuit graduation ceremony leading article lift pedestrian crossing ESL と EFL を明確に区別する autumn first-year student / fresher second-year student third-year student fourth-year student petrol station go on holiday bonnet car park general manager ill the ground floor platform lorry
語義	home は「家庭」「家（建物）」を指す toilet は「便器」を指す college が大学を総称する	home は「家庭」のみを指す toilet は「トイレの部屋全体」を指す college と university を明確に区別する
文法	anytime to tell you the truth Do you have a pen? I have gone to Tokyo twice. I forgot my phone in the car. Should we go now? learned dreamed burned gotten from Monday through Friday	at any time / any time to tell the truth Have you got a pen? I have been to Tokyo twice. I left my phone in the car. Shall we go now? learned / learnt dreamed / dreamt burned / burnt got from Monday to Friday

Web動画のご案内　StreamLine

本テキストの映像は、オンラインでのストリーミング再生になります。下記URLよりご利用ください。なお**有効期限は、はじめてログインした時点から1年半**です。

http://st.seibido.co.jp

1 ログイン画面

テキストに添付されているシールをはがして、12桁のアクセスコードをご入力ください。

同意してログイン

以下の「利用規約」をご確認頂き、同意する場合は上記ボタン【同意してログイン】を押してください。

利用規約

1. このウェブサイト（以下「本サイト」といいます）は、株式会社成美堂（以下「弊社」といいます）が運営しています。弊社の商品・サービス（以下「本サービス」といいます）利用時の会員登録の有無を問わず、本サイトの利用にあたっては、以下のご利用条件をお読み頂き、これらの条件にご同意の上ご利用ください。

2. 本サービスに関して個別に利用規約がある場合、本規約に加えそれらも適用されます。

3. 本サイトを通じて、弊社の商品を販売する第三者のウェブサイトにご案内ないしリンクされることがあります。リンク先ウェブサイトにおいて提供された個人情報は

巻末に添付されているシールをはがして、アクセスコードをご入力ください。

2 メニュー画面

AFP World Focus
–Environment, Health, and Technology–
アクセスコード有効期限：2018年4月30日

Video　Audio

- Lesson 1: Global Warming and Climat…
- Lesson 2: Diet and Health for Long …
- Lesson 3: Self-Driving for the Futu…
- Lesson 4: Sustaining Biodiversity a…
- Lesson 5: 3D Printers for Creating …
- Lesson 6: IT and Education
- Lesson 7: Protection from Natural D…
- Lesson 8: Practical Uses of Drones …

「Video」または「Audio」を選択すると、それぞれストリーミング再生ができます。

3 再生画面

AFP World Focus
–Environment, Health, and Technology–
アクセスコード有効期限：2018年4月30日

Lesson 2:
Diet and Health for Long Lives
食習慣：長生きのためのスーパーフードを探す

推奨動作環境

【PC OS】
Windows 7~ / Mac 10.8~

【Mobile OS】
iOS / Android ※Android の場合は4.x~が推奨

【Desktop ブラウザ】
Internet Explorer 9~ / Firefox / Chrome / Safari

TEXT PRODUCTION STAFF

edited by	編集
Masato Kogame	小亀 正人
cover design by	表紙デザイン
Nobuyoshi Fujino	藤野 伸芳

CD PRODUCTION STAFF

recorded by	吹き込み者
Jennifer Okano (AmE)	ジェニファー・オカノ（アメリカ英語）
Dominic Allen (AmE)	ドミニク・アレン（アメリカ英語）
Karen Haedrich(AmE)	カレン・ヘドリック（アメリカ英語）
Howard Colefield (AmE)	ハワード・コルフィールド（アメリカ英語）

Reuters Global News Feed
ロイターニュースが伝える世界の今

2025年1月20日　初版発行
2025年2月15日　第2刷発行

著　者　小林 敏彦
Bill Benfield

発行者　佐野 英一郎

発行所　株式会社 成 美 堂
〒101-0052東京都千代田区神田小川町3-22
TEL 03-3291-2261　FAX 03-3293-5490
https://www.seibido.co.jp

印刷・製本　萩原印刷株式会社

ISBN 978-4-7919-7311-8　Printed in Japan